Joseph C. Sweeney

THE PEOPLE INTO PARLIAMENT

'Labours first May Day.' Cartoon by Walter Crane, 1889

The People into Parliament

A CONCISE HISTORY OF
THE LABOUR MOVEMENT IN BRITAIN

W. T. RODGERS AND BERNARD DONOUGHUE

with 235 illustrations

A STUDIO BOOK

THE VIKING PRESS · NEW YORK

ACKNOWLEDGEMENTS

The authors are particularly grateful to Mr Philip Williams, Fellow of Nuffield College, Oxford, for reading the text and making many helpful suggestions; and to the publisher's editor Miss Ann Stevens for picture research

Contents

The cover of *Fabian Essays in Socialism*, 1889, edited by George Bernard Shaw and destined to have a lasting influence

Chapter One

THE SOCIALIST AWAKENING

During the thirty years after the Great Exhibition of 1851 Britain was unrivalled as the workshop of the world. The continued decline of agriculture was matched by the growth of the urban population and rapid expansion in cotton, coal, iron and steel, and ship-building. Industrial output as a whole rose by over three per cent a year. Despite appalling conditions and extreme poverty amongst sections of the community, the prosperity of mid-Victorian England rubbed off on all classes. Rising prices during most of the period were more than offset by rising wages. After pressure from the unions, the working day was reduced in a number of trades. At least until the mid-1870s this was an age of growing affluence in which everyone's standard of living showed a marked improvement.

Legislation was also creating new opportunities. The 1870 Education Act led to compulsory schooling for all children: knowledge as well as thrift was a virtue to which everyone could now aspire. The Reform Act of 1867 almost doubled the electorate, giving the vote to the urban working class, and in 1884 the franchise was extended to the counties, and thus in principle to virtually the whole of the adult male population. The Public Health Act of 1875 laid down standards which were to survive for many years and much minor legislation extended the sphere of state responsibility for welfare. Disraeli and

Signs of the time: a broadsheet of 1867 celebrates electoral reform, and below, Mr Forster surveys some of the ragged children whom his Act of 1870 would send to school

THE THREE R's; OR, BETTER LATE THAN NEVER.

RIGHT HON. W. E. FORSTER (CHAIRMAN OF BOARD). "WELL, MY LITTLE PEOPLE, WE HAVE BEEN GRAVELY AND EARNESTLY CONSIDERING WHETHER YOU MAY LEARN TO READ. I AM HAPPY TO TELL YOU THAT, SUBJECT TO A VARIETY OF RESTRICTIONS, CONSCIENCE CLAUSES, AND THE CONSENT OF YOUR VESTRIES—YOU MAY!"

Peabody Square, Westminster, 'for the dwellings of the poor', another monument to the awakening social conscience of Victorian England

Gladstone each formed his first Cabinet in 1868 and their rivalries dominated the Parliamentary scene.

As Queen Victoria's reign approached its Diamond Jubilee, it was easy to believe in the comfortable inevitability of progress. England was rich, democratic and at peace with the world. What could possibly ruffle her calm self-assurance?

The socialist awakening did not, at first, do so. The formation of the Democratic Federation in 1881 – which became the Social Democratic Federation (SDF) three years later – and of the Fabian Society in 1884 passed unsung. Neither looked the forerunner of a movement which could challenge the established bastions of political power. But in fact the SDF and the Fabian Society were to play a significant part in arousing socialist opinion; and the Fabians were to make an enduring contribution to the politics of the left.

The beginnings of social protest, 1381: John Ball rides to meet Wat Tyler

An earlier tradition of protest

The movement of social protest in England had, of course, a long and distinguished tradition. Five centuries before, in 1381, John Ball had died on the gallows at St Albans at the end of the Peasants' Revolt against the injustice inflicted by changes in the social order with the break-up of feudalism. 'When Adam delved and Eve span', he asked, 'who was then the gentleman?' The simple agrarian socialists of medieval times found successors in the 'Diggers' of Cromwell's day. Before it turned sour, the English Revolution inspired a ferment of ideas about the social question. The 'Agreement of the People', put forward by John Lilburne and the Levellers, opposed economic and social privilege and demanded manhood suffrage for free citizens. Colonel Thomas Rainborowe of Cromwell's army expressed the radical mood: 'The poorest he that is in England hath a life to lead as the greatest he.'

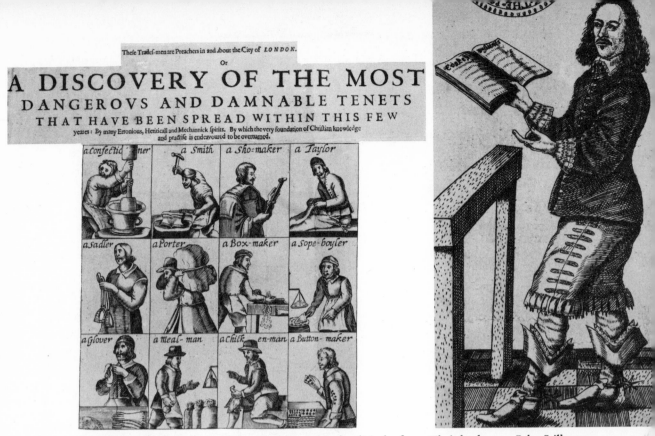

The Levellers of Cromwell's day pressed the case for social and political reform. Their leader was John Lilburne

But the inspiration and origins of the successful demand for govern-ment both by and in the interests of the people as a whole are to be found later. From about 1760 onwards, and particularly from 1780, a great transformation took place in the economic life of Britain which was substantially completed by the time Queen Victoria ascended the throne in 1837. The invention of new machines and processes – the 'Spinning Jenny' of James Hargreaves, the water frame of Richard Arkwright, the iron 'puddling' process of Henry Cort – was a prelude to rapid industrial expansion in which the steam engine played an increasingly central part. The growth of banking and exports in the 1780s was followed by a remarkable expansion in the iron industry under the stimulus of the French wars. The output of pig-iron rose four-fold in twenty years and contributed to a similar rise in coal

The Industrial Revolution

13

The opening of the Stockton and Darlington railway in 1825, heralding the second

The Railway Age mining. The peak years of canal building between 1790 and 1810 gave way to a period of road improvement and then, from the opening of the Stockton and Darlington line in 1825, to the great railway age. The population grew at an unprecedented rate. In 1760 the population of England, Wales and Scotland together was probably less than eight million. By the first census in 1801 it was nearly eleven million and by 1811 twelve and a half million, a rate of increase maintained through out the century. The new population crowded into the towns. London grew from three-quarters of a million in 1760 to over a million by 1811. Manchester, Edinburgh, Glasgow, Liverpool, Birmingham, Bristol

stage of the Industrial Revolution

Impressions of town
and country life in
the 1870s

and Leeds all added well over ten per cent to their population between 1801 and 1811. Although agriculture remained by far the largest employer and there was little rural depopulation, a great change nevertheless took place in the relative importance of industry and agriculture, of town life and country life. The settled pattern of centuries was disrupted, creating economic problems and social tensions and an environment in which new political movements could grow. This industrial revolution was of more lasting importance than the radical ideas born out of the influence of the French Revolution. It was decisive in creating the conditions for socialism.

15

Trade union struggles   The most significant evidence of new cross-currents amongst the working class was the development of the trade unions, the beginnings of the Co-operative movement and the phenomenon of the Chartist movement.

The Combination Acts, passed in 1799 and 1800 ostensibly to check seditious activities, were repealed in 1824. Repeal, and a new Act passed the following year, freed the trade unions from actions for criminal conspiracy. In the eighteenth century they had been loose associations of skilled craftsmen, coming together to provide 'friendly society' benefits and to regulate the conditions of their trade – coopers, plumbers, painters, joiners, sailmakers, hatters, millwrights. Now, no longer outlawed, trade unionism began to grow. Local trade clubs, characteristic of the earlier period, joined together in regional and national associations. Despite the sentence of transportation passed on

Early unions like the Felt-makers, whose emblem is shown here, were loose associations of skilled craftsmen

George Odger, centre, a leading member of the London Trades Council and Secretary of the TUC in 1871, was an early trade union candidate for Parliament

16

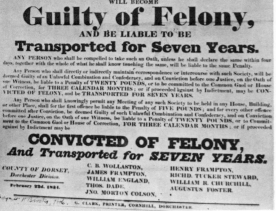

The Tolpuddle 'martyrs' were victims of the trade union struggle for recognition. (*Left*) The notice posted at Tolpuddle two days before the arrest of the six labourers. (*Above*) An impression of the Trade Union demonstration against the sentences of deportation

six farm labourers at Tolpuddle in Dorset in 1834 for swearing illegal oaths, and the collapse in the same years of the massive Grand National Consolidated Trades Union, the trade unions felt their way towards better organization and more settled ways.

Working men also found an outlet for self-help in the Co-operative movement. In the first phase, in the late 1820s and early 1830s, the belief of Robert Owen in the virtue of co-operative production and co-operative communities was the driving force. Convinced by his experience as an enlightened mill-owner at Lanark in Scotland of the influence of environment on individual character, he hoped that co-operation would replace capitalism and put an end to poverty. In the second, less Utopian phase, the hardheaded Rochdale Pioneers of 1844 and their successors took the ideal of Owenite co-operation and applied it to retail trade. The Co-operative movement thereafter grew steadily, a monument to the practical virtues and enterprise of ordinary people and a training ground for the administrators and committee men of a wider working-class movement.

Co-operation

Robert Owen

In 1842 Chartists marched in a great procession to the House of Commons to present their National Petition for a second time

Fergus O'Connor

Chartism
    The history of Chartism is shorter and more dramatic. Chartism, which flourished mainly in the decade 1838–48, was a fierce and sometimes violent protest of working men against industrial conditions and exclusion from political life. The 'People's Charter', drawn up by a journeyman cabinet-maker, William Lovett, of the London Working Men's Association, had six main points – adult male suffrage, voting by secret ballot, equal Parliamentary constituencies, annual Parliaments, no property qualification for MPs and Parliamentary salaries. A National Petition for reform, originating in the Birmingham Political Union, was three times presented to Parliament – in 1839, 1842 and 1848 – and at its peak the movement brought together a wide variety of radicals and revolutionaries into both legal and seditious activity. But there were quarrels in the leadership between moderates like Lovett and violent demagogues like Feargus O'Connor and the extreme advocates of physical force; as a result the movement

finally fizzled out in abortive land reform schemes, riots and disillusionment.

Between these and other working-class movements of the 1830s and 1840s and the events of the 1880s there were few links, except through the survival into old age of some of the participants. There was no continuity between Chartism, the most ideological of them, and the socialist organizations of late Victorian England. Yet in a real sense they showed many of the characteristics of the Labour Movement in the motives which led to their growth, in the allegiance they won, in their composition and in their ideals. A later generation could look back on them as the forerunners.

A Chartist-organized 'sit-in' in Church, involving filling the pews early, wearing hats and smoking pipes

Karl Marx

The 1880 General Election gave Gladstone a handsome victory over Disraeli and the Conservatives. It also saw the defeat in the St Marylebone constituency of the Tory candidate H. M. Hyndman. Hyndman, a well-to-do journalist educated at Eton and Cambridge, was then rapidly converted to socialism by reading Karl Marx's *Capital*. By June 1881 he was ready to take a leading part in the inaugural conference of the Democratic Federation and to become its President. The new organization aimed at bringing together numerous tiny radical societies into a new political party capable of representing the working class. Meetings were held in support of Irish Home Rule, Parliamentary reform and a shorter working day; branches were set up and a newspaper published. The nationalization of the means of production, distribution and exchange was adopted as a programme after its change of name in 1884. The public debates in which Hyndman took part helped to publicize the new socialism. The leadership of the SDF was middle-class but it was able to mobilize popular support for its activities. Over one thousand people were said to have taken part in a procession to the grave of Karl Marx in Highgate, London, in March 1884, the first anniversary of his death.

The Social Democratic Federation's unemployment rally in 1886 led to the breaking of windows in the clubs of Pall Mall

The Social Democratic Federation's leaders: Jack Williams, H. M. Hyndman, H. H. Champion, and John Burns sit in Court following the disturbances. They were eventually acquitted at the Old Bailey

Sporadically arousing public opinion was one thing; providing the organization necessary to permanent success was another. During its existence the SDF did much to carry the name of socialism to places where otherwise it would have gone unheard. Under the influence of the SDF working men educated themselves to make the case for socialism, of whatever variety. A *cadre* of advocates was created who played an active part in propagating the new ideas in the barren years of Liberal and Conservative supremacy. Especially in the North of England, old SDF members could be found still staunchly loyal to their persuasion in the second half of the twentieth century. George Lansbury, a future leader of the Labour Party, served his apprenticeship as an SDF propagandist; Will Thorne, who became first Secretary of the Gasworkers was a prominent member.

The contribution of the SDF in the 1880s and the 1890s was important. It was not, however, decisive in determining the course of events. Disagreements in the leadership were constant. For a year or

The membership card of the SDF, designed by William Morris

LIBERTY EQUALITY FRATERNITY

EDUCATE   ORGANISE

DEMOCRATIC FEDERATION

AGITATE

two William Morris was a member, acting as Treasurer and adding distinction to its journal *Justice*, but he fell out with Hyndman and went off to form the Socialist League. Another break followed the acceptance, in 1885, of £340 from the Conservatives (who hoped to split the Liberal vote) towards the election expenses of two Parliamentary candidates. 'Tory gold' was too much to stomach and Hyndman earned his unpopularity; nor was his personality ever conducive to unity.

An unemployment rally in Trafalgar Square in February 1886 led to a march through London and the breaking of windows in the clubs of Pall Mall. It was effective publicity, but proved no substitute in the long run for the hard, often unspectacular work of organization. As for the political views of the SDF, Hyndman, although disowned by Marx himself, was a committed Marxist, believing in the total collapse of capitalist society and in the triumph of revolutionary socialism. For tactical purposes the SDF put up Parliamentary candidates although political action was rejected as a permanent solution to the problem of working-class emancipation. But by the second half of the 1880s class war already seemed to many a doubtful proposition. The exercise of the vote which working men now possessed promised

(*Left*) William Morris. (*Below, left to right*) *Justice*, the Social Democratic Federation's Journal; Membership card of the Socialist League, Hammersmith, and the Socialist League Manifesto

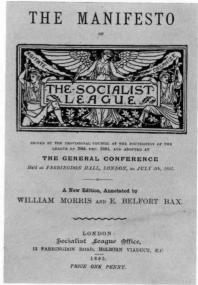

The Socialist League, Hammersmith, formerly a branch of the SDF, with William Morris fourth from the right in the second row

reforms by constitutional means. The real question was whether pressure on the existing parties would do the trick.

The circumstances in which the Democratic Federation was created were inauspicious. The beginnings of the Fabian Society were even more obscure. Its origins lay in a visit to London in 1883 of Thomas Davidson, a Scot who had settled in America but spent much of his time in Europe lecturing, writing and founding ethical societies. As a result, a small group came together in rooms off Regents Park and launched the Fellowship of the New Life, dedicated to 'the cultivation of a perfect character' and the 'subordination of material things to spiritual'. This, however, was too Utopian for some of its sympathizers and a rift occurred. A further aim was then adopted: because the competitive system assured 'the happiness and comfort of the few at the expense of the suffering of the many', society 'must be reconstituted in such a manner as to secure the general welfare and happiness'. This

The Fabian Society

23

George Bernard Shaw in 1885

Sidney Webb in 1898

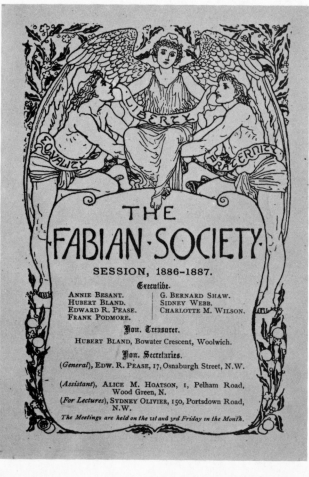

The Fabian Society's programme for 1886–7

was the basis upon which the Fabian Society was launched on 4 January 1884. It was not explicitly socialist but henceforth Fabian activities were socialist in all but name. The first Fabian tract, *Why are the many poor?*, appeared in April 1884, and it was primarily in pamphleteering that the Society was to make and maintain its reputation.

Unlike the delegates to the first meeting of the SDF, the founders of the Fabian Society had no representative standing, and none was a public figure or played a central part in the subsequent history of socialism (two, in fact, had met ghost-hunting in a house at Notting Hill Gate). What soon gave the Society its strength and impetus was the adherence of George Bernard Shaw and Sidney Webb. In January 1884, Shaw was writing unsuccessful novels and living with (and off) his mother and sisters a few doors away from the rooms where the Fabians met. By September he was a member and had written his first pamphlet, *A Manifesto*. It set forth in typically epigrammatic style the opinions which Fabians shared: *Shaw and Webb*

> That under existing circumstances wealth cannot be enjoyed without dishonour or forgone without misery.
>
> That the most striking result of our present system of farming out the national Land and Capital to private persons has been the division of Society into hostile classes, with large appetites and no dinners at one extreme and large dinners and no appetites at the other.
>
> That the established Government has no more right to call itself the State than the smoke of London to call itself the weather.

If Shaw was to prove a superb propagandist, it was Sidney Webb who was to give the Society its name for social research and pragmatic policy-making. Introduced by Shaw, he joined the following year when he was a clerk in the Colonial Office. Together they provided the intellectual leadership of the Fabians for many years.

Shaw later described the Society when he joined it as 'a silly business. They had one elderly retired workman. They had two psychical researchers. . . . There were Anarchists. . . . There were young ladies on the lookout for husbands who left when they succeeded.' But it soon began to attract men and women of considerable talent. Its private conferences and drawing-room meetings were in sharp contrast to the vigorous public activities of the SDF – by which it was viewed with suspicion. Not only its leadership but its growing membership was overwhelmingly middle-class. It was open to criticism as being remote from the mainstream of working-class politics, an intellectual coterie, principally enjoying talk for talk's sake. But the discussions of this group of thoughtful socialists were at least as relevant to the mode and needs of the time as the propaganda of the SDF.

After a brief period of uncertainty the Fabians became resolute constitutionalists, determined to transform society by democratic means. They recognized that the process might be slow but believed that if facts were collected and the case clearly argued the cause could be won. Patient social engineering was a surer passport to success than revolutionary ardour. The Fabians were never dogmatic in requiring their members to affirm support for a narrow definition of socialism. But from 1887 onwards, Fabian socialism was gradualist, based upon persuasion and the 'permeation' of society and institutions with socialist ideas.

'Fabian Essays' What put the Society on the map was the publication of *Fabian Essays in Socialism* in 1889. The book was based on a series of lectures given the previous year and was edited by Shaw. It astounded its authors by selling one thousand copies within a month and over twenty thousand within two years. Shaw claimed that the essayists were only 'communicative learners' – as good a description as any of how the Fabians have subsequently seen themselves. They drew their ideas from a number of different sources: the utilitarians, classical economists, the early socialists and Marx. But they stated clearly their belief in democracy as the means to socialism. Important changes in society, wrote Sidney Webb, could only be '(1) democratic and thus acceptable to a majority of the people . . .; (2) gradual, and thus causing no dislocation, however rapid may be the rate of progress; (3) not regarded as immoral by the mass of the people . . .; and (4) in this country, at any rate, constitutional and peaceful.'

26

'The Webb of Destiny.' *Punch* makes fun of socialism. 'Mr Sidney Webb: I am waving this red flag not provocatively but to signalize what I have so happily called "the inevitability of gradualness" which marks our roller's advance.'

This was to be an essential element in the kind of socialism adopted by the Labour Party. There would be times when faith in democracy and 'the inevitability of gradualness' (a phrase of Sidney Webb's from later years) would undergo strain; within the Labour Party the Fabian approach would meet constant criticism from the heirs to the revolutionary socialist tradition. But to the democratic process and to winning power by consent British socialism was to become firmly committed.

Apart from the SDF and the Fabian Society there were many small groups, like the Christian Socialist Guild of St Matthew, on the periphery of socialist politics. But as an historian of the period has said, 'the Socialists were a sort of "stage army" in the 1880s. There were plenty of leaders anxious to play eloquent and dramatic parts; but the supporting cast, being very limited, had to make up for their lack of numbers by frequent changes of role.'

27

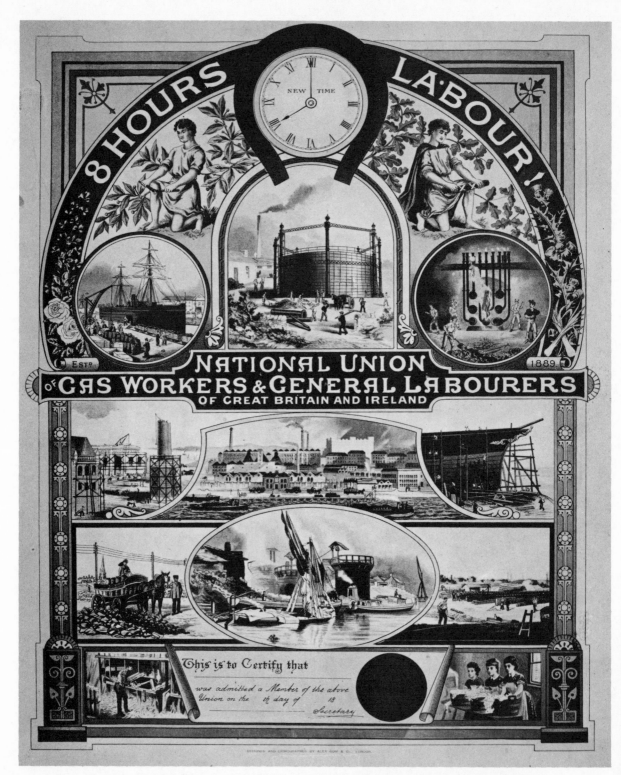

In 1889 victory of the Gas Workers and General Labourers in their campaign for an
eight-hour day heralded a new phase of more militant trade unionism

Chapter Two

WINNING SUPPORT

In 1889, however, there were sudden developments in the trade union world. Since the middle of the century there had been considerable growth in the membership and influence of a number of well-established trade unions, checked only in times of trade depression. By 1888 the Amalgamated Society of Engineers, founded in 1851, had 54,000 members and the Carpenters and Joiners, founded in 1860, had 25,000. From 1860, the London Trades Council was an important influence amongst the artisans of the capital, and in 1868 the Trades Union Congress (TUC) was formally established and three years later set up a Parliamentary Committee. In 1875 the Conspiracy and Protection of Property Act legalized peaceful picketing.

Many trade unionists played an active part in the movement for Parliamentary reform. The building trades were particularly militant and George Potter, their London leader, founded the *Beehive*, the most successful working-class newspaper of the mid-nineteenth century. In 1874 Thomas Burt and Alexander Macdonald, both miners, were elected to Parliament, the first working-class Members. They were joined in 1880 by Henry Broadhurst, Secretary of the TUC, and by 1885 the number of working-class MPs had risen to eleven.

Then in March 1889 Will Thorne, a stoker at the Becton, London, works of the South Metropolitan Gas Company and a member of the

Will Thorne

Ben Tillett

Tom Mann

SDF, launched the National Union of Gas Workers and General Labourers with an eight-hour day as its principal objective. Within three months the demand had been met by the major London companies and an attempt at victimization had failed. Thorne was elected General Secretary of the new union which, in the following year, spread throughout the country. In 1890 it affiliated to the TUC on the basis of 60,000 members and although its growth was soon checked, it eventually became the massive National Union of General and Municipal Workers of today, with three-quarters of a million members.

The 'Docker's Tanner'

The establishment of the other new union of 1889 was even more dramatic. A dispute in the South West India Dock on 12 August provided a pretext for a major confrontation with the dock employers. Since 1887 Ben Tillett's Tea Operatives and General Labourers Association had been attempting to organize the dockers, and it now led a strike for a wage rate of 'a tanner', 6d an hour – instead of the 4d (at Tilbury) or 5d then paid. The chance of success seemed small, despite the hopeful example of the gasworkers. But skilful leadership from Tillett, John Burns and Tom Mann, the enthusiasm of the dockers, support from the existing unions of stevedores which provided experienced key-workers, active help from members of the SDF, almost £50,000 in donations, and, not least, widespread public sympathy, created a totally unexpected situation. Daily marches from the East End through London to Hyde Park, led by John Burns and facilitated by

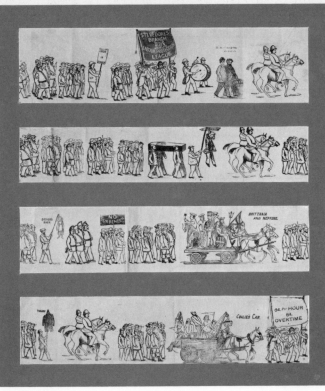

(*Above*) John Burns speaks in Hyde Park

(*Above left*) Part of the crocodile programme issued by the Dockers' Union at the time of its East End marches for the 'Docker's Tanner'. The police head the procession, followed by John Burns and H.H. Champion, then the stevedores' band and 'the multitude whose calling lay at the docks'

(*Below*) Dockers hopefully waiting the result of their demand

the friendly attitude of the police, drew attention to the dockers' conditions of life. A Mansion House Committee which included the Lord Mayor and Cardinal Manning – who played an important part in achieving a settlement – was set up for the purpose of conciliation and even *The Times* was sympathetic in its attitude. From their headquarters in the Wade's Arms at Poplar, the strikers made their case for the 'Docker's Tanner' and received financial help from as far away as Australia. After a month, and a period of crisis in the middle of it when the issue was in doubt, the strike was won. The employers conceded 6d an hour and membership of the union was recognized as essential for London dock workers. Dockers were rapidly organized in other parts of the country either by Tillett's own union or by the National Union of Dock Labourers, which together affiliated to the T U C on the basis of over 100,000 members. As with the gasworkers, this initial success was not sustained, but in later years, having recruited Ernest Bevin as an organizer, the dockers went on to form the nucleus of the other great general union, the Transport and General Workers.

The New Unionism   The new unions were seen to be more militant and more widely representative of labour than those already well-established. With low subscription rates they organized the relatively unskilled and were open to all those willing to join. Their leaders were politically conscious and in touch with the socialist movement. In retrospect, it is perhaps less clear that they were so distinctive.

What matters is that the 'new unionism' brought into the trade union movement thousands of men previously outside it and in so doing gave a push to wider working-class organization.

The Mansion House conciliation committee included the Lord Mayor of London and Cardinal Manning

Blatchford's *Clarion*, at the height of its popularity

Thus as the 1890s opened it was clear that the time had come for a new and bolder initiative. The SDF and the Fabians, for all their limitations, had created a ferment of ideas absent a decade before. In addition, with the advent of the new unionism, a slumbering giant seemed to have been awakened. The socialists and the trade unions had members in common. Socialist leaders had fulfilled a crucial role in the events of 1889; even Edward Pease, the Fabian secretary, had played a part in the organization of the Tyneside National Labour Federation, a forerunner of the new unionism.

A number of factors contributed to the growth of political activity in the North of England and particularly in Lancashire and Yorkshire. The Fabians were responsible for a campaign in Lancashire in the autumn of 1889 during which sixty lectures were given in Liberal and Radical clubs, and to Co-operative societies and branches of the SDF and Socialist League. But even more significant was an indigenous wave of interest. From Manchester the persuasive voice of Robert Blatchford was to be heard, first as a journalist on the *Sunday Chronicle* and then as editor of his own paper, *The Clarion*. The exuberant propaganda of

Robert Blatchford

Handbills pleading for and against the strike at the Manningham Mills in Bradford 1891, a symptom of the growing militancy of the North

Militancy in the North

The Clarion spread out from Manchester, where an independent labour party was established bringing together many local groups. In Bradford, as a result of a bitter industrial dispute at the Manningham Mills, a Labour Union was formed, pledged to political action. Blatchford and Ben Tillett, the dockers' leader, were invited to become Parliamentary candidates in the General Election of 1892 and Tillett, standing for West Bradford, came within a few hundred votes of winning. In the country as a whole, with one or two exceptions, independent working-class candidates did less well.

The most notable exception was James Keir Hardie, who won South West Ham. Keir Hardie was a Fabian but of a different stamp from the leadership of the Society, which at that time had no high opinion of

Keir Hardie, left, with George Bernard Shaw and Shaw's wife

him: to Shaw he was 'a Scotsman with alternate intervals of second *Keir Hardie* sight and common incapacity'. Hardie's origins were among the miners of Lanarkshire and his story is a central part of the history of the Labour movement.

Keir Hardie was born in 1856, the illegitimate son of a farm servant. He started work at the age of eight and grew up in acute poverty. He became active in the Temperance Movement and was then drawn into trade union work. Moving from Liberalism towards socialism, influenced by the SDF but rejecting what he regarded as unconstructive factionalism, he erupted on the TUC in 1887 as a militant advocate of independent labour politics. Six months later he was the miners' nominee in the mid-Lanark by-election and although he finished bottom of the poll he opened up the whole question of independent working-class representation in Parliament. The formation of the Scottish Labour Party followed in August 1888. It was his victory at West Ham, however, which put him firmly on the political map. Arriving at Westminster in a cloth cap and tweed jacket, he pursued from the beginning a policy of independence, refusing to sit on the Government (Liberal) benches and seeking every opportunity to raise questions affecting labour interests.

The Independent Labour Party

Hardie was still only one of many equal leaders of a fragmented socialist movement. But he was the natural candidate for chairman when in September 1892 a preliminary meeting was held in Glasgow to organize a national conference with a view to forming an independent labour party. This conference was held in the Bradford Labour Institute on 13 and 14 January 1893. There were delegates from the S D F, the Fabian Society, the Scottish Labour Party, the trade unions and, more important in terms of enthusiasm, many local socialist groups and labour clubs. Delegates were mostly from the North of England. The success amongst working-class readers of the weekly *Yorkshire Factory Times*, the existence of many small trade unions, educational and co-operative bodies, even the survival of memories of Chartist days – all

Despite inauspicious beginnings in 1893 the ILP survived to celebrate its coming of age

Hardie's clothes caused a stir amidst the
sober formality of Westminster

Keir Hardie's membership card

these made the West Riding a fertile soil for support. The parent Fabian
Society of London was represented by two delegates, one of whom was
Shaw, but delegates were sent by eleven local Fabian societies, some
of which had been established during the 1889 Lancashire campaign.
Despite the attendance of such established leaders as Hardie, Tillett
and Blatchford, the strength of the Conference was in the anonymous
rank and file.

Its hope for the future also lay in securing the sympathy and support
of trade unions. Tillett made clear that he 'wished to capture the trade
unionists of this country, a body of men well organized, who paid their
money and were socialists at their work every day and not merely on the
platform'. The emphasis in the programme the Conference adopted was
on practical objectives – the eight-hour day, provision for sickness and
old age, free education and the abolition of indirect taxation. But the
socialist basis of the new party was defined in its commitment to the
collective ownership of the means of production, distribution and

37

exchange. In the eyes of its founders, the Independent Labour Party (ILP) was to be a non-doctrinaire party of practical socialists, providing the organization for winning Parliamentary representation for the working man.

The Conference had been a success. The Fabians were mildly sceptical about the future of the ILP and the SDF was critical of its failure to take a more whole-hogging socialist stance. Blatchford was impatient of the compromises necessary to build up a soundly based political party. But the decision had been made: the working man would seek to enter politics directly and on his own account.

The Liberal dilemma
The idea of working-class representation was not new but in the recent past the accepted vehicle had been the Liberal Party. When, in 1869, a prospect of direct representation in Parliament was first discussed at the TUC, its main advocate, a former Chartist, nevertheless anticipated that representation would be under the Liberal umbrella.

The predominance of the miners in certain parts of the country enabled them to impose their candidates on the Liberal Party and in practice no working-class MP was returned except by grace of the Liberals. In the mid-Lanark by-election of 1888, even Keir Hardie had fought under the banner 'a vote for Hardie is a vote for Gladstone'. The Newcastle Programme adopted by the Liberal Party in 1891 was radical. Shaw, a member of the St Pancras Liberal and Radical Association, claimed that he and Sidney Webb were indirectly responsible for its drafting. The Fabians certainly did not reject the Liberal Party as a

By adopting a new programme of reforms at Newcastle in 1891, the Liberal Party hoped to win Labour votes

vehicle for reform. Even the Bradford conference agreed, after an argument, that members of the ILP should be free to support other candidates in the absence of a socialist. Few leaders of the Labour and Socialist movement were willing to turn their backs firmly on the Liberal Party; and if the Liberals had shown less reluctance to adopt working-class candidates in the country as a whole, they might still have prevented the growth of independant labour representation. As it was, the coming years witnessed many shifts and manœuvres before confidence was complete that the Liberal Party should be confronted without reservation and might one day be replaced.

Slow growth

The establishment of the ILP did not immediately transform the political scene. On the contrary, socialist progress was slow. At the 1895 General Election there were twenty-eight ILP candidates and four supported by the SDF, but none was successful. At South West Ham, Keir Hardie himself was defeated. A new recruit to the Party, James Ramsay MacDonald, polled fewer than 900 votes at Southampton and criticized Hardie's 'incapacity'. The following year, in a by-election at East Bradford, Hardie was bottom of the poll in a three-cornered fight. Membership of the ILP was small and remained concentrated in the North of England. The SDF fared no better. Personal differences and doctrinal disputes reduced its influence and although useful propaganda continued there were no signs of growth.

Only the Fabians had some modest progress to show. After 1893, many local Fabian societies were absorbed into branches of the ILP.

The ILP's attitude as seen by the *Westminster Gazette* of July 1895

Mr. K— H—: "Can't get in myself, but I can keep a few others out, anyway."

An election edition of the weekly *Labour Leader*, a paper edited by Keir Hardie

The focus of Fabian activity was London and the emphasis was on local government. In 1889, the year in which the London County Council was founded, Tract 8, *Facts for Londoners* was published. In the next ten years, a majority of pamphlets dealt with local government, some fifty in all. There were lists of searching questions to be put to Poor Law Guardians, vestrymen and candidates for school boards, town councils and county councils; and pamphlets on the municipalization of gas supply, tramways, docks and water. In 1892 Sidney Webb was elected to the LCC as one of six Fabians and took an active part in the loose group of progressives, becoming Chairman of the important Technical Education Board. *The London Programme* of 1892, written by Webb, set out to rouse the conscience of Londoners:

St Pancras workhouse in 1900, the able-bodied together with the old and frail

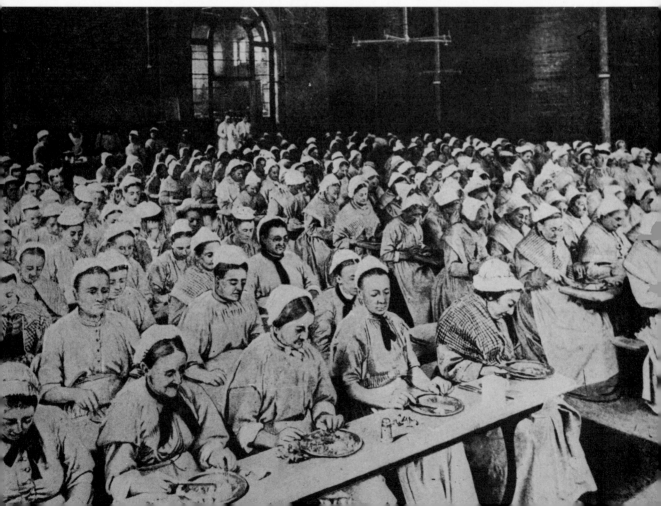

A new ward for the 'casual poor' at St Marylebone workhouse

Twenty thousand of its citizens fight in the fearful daily struggle for bread at the dock gates . . . Thirty thousand of its children are at school entirely breakfastless. One of every five of the five millions who began again today the weary round of life will eventually quit that life in the workhouse or the hospital . . . And all this in the richest and most productive city in the world, paying an annual tribute, or ground rent, of fifteen millions sterling for mere permission to occupy the low hills and among marsh by the Thames which labour alone has rendered productive!

Throughout the 1890s lectures were also given by prominent Fabians at many Liberal and Radical Working Men's Clubs. The slow process of socialist education continued.

London match-girls employed by Bryant and May's struck successfully in 1888 against cruel conditions of work

It was Robert Blatchford and *The Clarion*, however, that provided the
most vigorous and enterprising socialist propaganda. There was no love
lost between Blatchford and Keir Hardie. From the beginning Blatchford was critical of the ILP's alliance with the trade unions and its
commitment to Parliamentary tactics. He thought Hardie 'vain, greedy,
crooked and bumptious'; and when Victor Grayson was elected to
Parliament in 1907, Blatchford regarded *him* as the first socialist MP.
But he had little sympathy either for the dogmatic Marxism of Hyndman. He was a romantic socialist, with a great love of humanity and
zest for life, disgusted by the squalor, ugliness and bigotry of an England
soured by industrialism and divided by class. He was not a practical
politician out to win power but a propagandist trying to arouse the
people from their apathy and make them socialists. His vehicle was
The Clarion and his most famous contribution was *Merrie England*, first
published as a series of open letters to 'John Smith of Oldham' in 1893.

Go out into the streets of any big English town, and use your
eyes, John. What do you find? You find some rich and idle, wasting
unearned wealth to their own shame and injury and the shame and
injury of others. You find hard-working people packed away in vile,
unhealthy streets. You find little children famished, dirty and half
naked outside the luxurious clubs, shops, hotels and theatres.

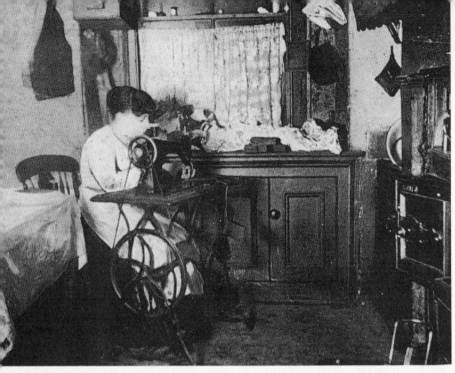

Sweated labour in Manchester in the 1890s. Slipper binding and closing at around a penny a pair

(*Above left*) Barefoot in the Liverpool slums. (*Right*) The cover of Blatchford's *Merrie England*

◀ Cycling was a phenomenon of great popularity in the 1890s. *Clarion* Cycle Clubs helped to increase the circulation of Blatchford's newspaper, and so the spread of socialist ideas

> You find men and women overworked and underpaid. You find want and disease cheek by jowl with religion and culture and wealth. You find the usurer, the gambler, the fop, the finnikin fine lady, and you find the starveling, the slave, the drunkard, and the harlot. Is it nothing to you, John Smith?

Published later as a shilling book, *Merrie England* eventually sold two million copies. *Clarion* Cycle Clubs and *Clarion* Scouts sold it on the doorsteps, at street corners and in the factories. *The Clarion*'s own circulation rose, helped also by *Clarion* Choirs, *Clarion* Handcraft Guilds and *Clarion* vans. Whatever the conflicts and rivalries in the leadership of the socialist movement, at the grass-roots converts were being made. The stage army was gaining recruits.

45

But despite trade union participation in the Bradford Conference, for the most part the unions whose growing strength the movement needed remained wary of independent political action. The cotton workers of Lancashire were predominantly Conservative and the miners were strong enough to promote their own candidates under the Liberal banner. The TUC's long-standing Parliamentary Committee was dominated by non-socialists. Only the new unions were active in support of the ILP. But from 1897, helped by tensions within their own industries, both the engineers and the railwaymen began to consider the need for independent working-class representation in Parliament, while members of the ILP were increasingly chosen as delegates to the Trades Union Congress. At the Congress of 1899 the Railway Servants put down a resolution to instruct the Parliamentary Committee

> to invite the co-operation of all the co-operative, socialistic, trade union, and other working organizations to jointly co-operate on lines mutually agreed upon, in convening a social congress of representatives from such above named organizations as may be willing to take part to devise ways and means for securing the return of an increased number of labour members to the next Parliament.

Support for this resolution was canvassed by the ILP (who may have had a hand in drafting it) and when put to the vote it was carried by 546,000 to 434,000. Representatives of the Parliamentary Committee, the Fabian Society, SDF and ILP then came together, agreed on an agenda and convened a Conference which met on 27 and 28 February 1900 in the Memorial Hall, Farringdon Street, London. This was to be the birthday and the birthplace of the Labour Party.

There were 129 delegates present. Seven, led by Hardie and Ramsay MacDonald, were from the ILP, four from the SDF and one from the Fabians. The remainder were trade unionists, although they represented less than a half of the 1,205,000 members affiliated to the TUC. It was not taken for granted that a majority would be easily found to support a new Parliamentary initiative or that there would be harmony between the strong personalities leading the delegations. In the event, the Conference went smoothly, largely because of the tactical skill of the I L P delegates who knew what they wanted. A proposal to limit the Parliamentary representatives of labour to 'members of the working classes' was defeated, John Burns declaring in an effective speech that the Conference 'should not be the prisoners of class prejudices'. But the most important resolution was moved by Keir Hardie and seconded on behalf of the Railway Servants. It proposed that there should be 'a distinct Labour Group in Parliament, who should have their own Whips and agree upon their policy. . . .'

Mr. JONES (representing Upholsterers) moved—"That this conference is in favour of the working-class opinion being represented in the House of Commons by members of the working classes, as being the most likely to be sympathetic with the aims and demands of the labour movement."

Mr. PAUL VOGEL (Waiters' Union) seconded.

Mr. GEORGE BARNES moved an amendment in favour of working-class opinion being represented "by men sympathetic with the aims of the labour movement, and whose candidatures are promoted by one or other of the organized movements represented at the conference."

Mr. JOHN BURNS, M.P., in seconding the amendment, said the resolution was narrow, intolerant, and exclusive. He was, he said, getting rather tired of hearing about workmen's boots, workmen's trains, workmen's dwellings, workmen's clothes, and working men candidates for working-class colonies. (Hear, hear.) The time had arrived in the history of the labour movement when they should no longer allow themselves to be prisoners to class phrases. (Laughter and "Hear. hear.") Did they propose to select boiler makers who earned £3 or £4 a week and reject clerks who dressed like dukes on the wages of dustmen ? (Laughter.) A navvy might be elected a Parliamentary representative, and if he became a great contractor would they reject him ?

The amendment was carried by 102 votes against 3.

The Parliamentary Committee submitted a resolution " in favour of establishing a distinct labour group in Parliament, who should have their own Whips and agree upon their policy, which must embrace a readiness to co-operate with any party which for the time being may be engaged in promoting legislation in the direct interest of labour, and be equally ready to associate themselves with any party in opposing measures having an opposite tendency," but in its place

Mr. JAMES MACDONALD moved—" The representatives of the working-class movement in the House of Commons shall form there a distinct party, with a party organization entirely separate from the capitalist parties, based upon a recognition of the class war, and having for its ultimate object the socialization of the means of production, distribution, and exchange ; the party shall formulate its own policy for promoting practical legislative measures in the interests of labour, and shall be prepared to co-operate with any party that will support such measures or will assist in opposing measures of an opposite character."

Part of *The Times* report of the Memorial Hall meeting of 1900, when representatives of the trade unions, the Fabian Society, the Social Democratic Federation and the I L P came together to form the Labour Representation Committee

47

This did not go far enough for the SDF, which preferred a statement that recognized the class war and called for the nationalization of the means of production, distribution and exchange. At the other extreme, the representative of the Shipwrights wanted a cautious agreement on limited aims which would not bind MPs. Hardie got his way: the need for organization was accepted and the demand for dogma turned down.

Other resolutions set up an Executive Committee of twelve, of whom two would come from the ILP, two from the SDF and one from the Fabians – a much higher proportion than the socialist organizations were entitled to on the basis of membership; and a central fund for administrative purposes, each body remaining responsible for financing its own candidates. The new Labour Representation Committee (LRC) was to call an annual conference and to prepare lists of official candidates before elections. Ramsay MacDonald was elected unpaid Secretary.

The Labour Representation Committee

Once again, the outlook for a new socialist organization was not good. Of the unions represented at the Memorial Hall, only a proportion joined, the engineers being amongst those who stayed out. The SDF was quick to condemn the ILP for 'treachery' for opposition to its 'class war' stand, complained that there could be 'no united party without unity of principle' (there being none) and withdrew from the LRC the following year. The Fabian Society showed comparatively little interest and, in the words of its own representative on the Executive, 'remained in a position of benevolent passivity'.

The results of the General Election in October 1900 did not, on the face of it, inspire hope of better prospects. The South African war, which broke out in 1899, and the jingoism that followed, was not favourable to the socialist movement. Blatchford, the ex-Army sergeant, was strenuous in support of the British Government's stand, and the Fabian Society was divided. But leaders of the ILP and SDF worked together in a 'Stop-the-War' movement and the TUC passed an anti-war resolution. With the tide of public opinion strongly hostile towards the pro-Boers, the way was open for the exploitation of patriotic sentiment against Labour candidates and their unpopular cause.

Scenes from the 1900 election in London. Working-class electors express their disapproval of some of the candidates and their canvassers

Richard Bell

Fifteen L R C candidates took the field, although moral support was the most the Committee could readily give as it had only £33 to spend on the whole election. Only two were successful, Richard Bell at Derby, in harness with a Liberal, and Keir Hardie at Merthyr, Wales as a whole being anti-war. In addition, the Liberal trade union M Ps – the 'Lib-Labs' – were reduced from twelve to eight.

One event really gave momentum to the L R C, and thereby had a decisive effect on the whole development of an independent Labour Movement. It had already occurred in August 1900, before the election,

Taff Vale but its consequences were at first obscured. Railwaymen on the Taff Vale line in South Wales struck for better conditions and to win recognition for their union. The strike was short and unsuccessful but the Taff Vale Company then claimed damages from the union, the Railway Servants. The case eventually went to the House of Lords where, in July 1901, judgment was given in the company's favour. The Railway Servants paid £23,000 damages and costs, and were out-of-pocket in all to almost twice this sum. The prospect opened up by the Taff Vale judgment was alarming. The whole strength of the trade unions, based on the ultimate sanction of the strike, was threatened. In future it seemed as if a legal action could be brought successfully against a union on account of any activity on the part of its officers or members involved in a trade dispute. The T U C, gravely concerned, found little support for new legislation outside the trade union movement. The Liberals were prepared to clarify the confusion caused by a complicated decision, but had not been eager to reverse it.

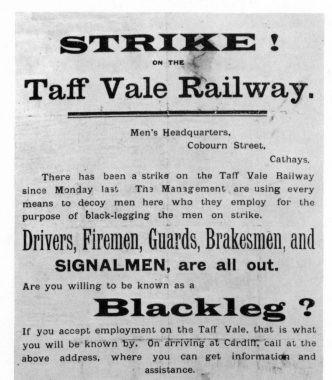

The Taff Vale case pushed the Unions into politics. Left, a strike poster, and above, the cheque for the twenty-three thousand pounds damages and costs subsequently awarded against the union

Arthur Henderson, centre, with his fellow foundry workers

Will Crooks, ex-Mayor of Poplar and LCC member, received Liberal support when he won Woolwich for Labour at a by-election in 1903

In these circumstances the unions turned to the LRC for help. A wave of new affiliations in 1902 raised trade union membership to 850,000; and the following year a compulsory levy was agreed to provide twenty-five per cent of the expenses of LRC candidates and £200 a year payment of MPs. It was anticipated that this would give the Committee greater control over LRC MPs who were now expected to form the 'distinct group' proposed in the Memorial Hall resolution. Meanwhile, by-elections resulted in the return of David Shackleton of the Weavers at Clitheroe, Will Crooks of the Coopers at Woolwich, and Arthur Henderson of the Ironfounders at Barnard Castle, all with LRC support, as well as two Lib-Labs. By the beginning of 1904, the LRC was impatient for the General Election.

By-election successes

One question which had become acute since 1900 was relations with the Liberal Party. It was apparent that LRC and Liberal candidates fighting against each other split the vote and generally let the Conservative in. The LRC was not happy at the thought of three-cornered contests and in 1903 the Liberals' own prospects were not good. An approach was therefore made by Ramsay MacDonald, with the

51

'The Ox and the Frog.' The Frog: 'I shall soon be bigger than you.' The Ox: 'All right, I don't mind, there's plenty of room for both of us – but mind you don't burst!'

A pact with the Liberals agreement of Keir Hardie, to Herbert Gladstone, the Liberal Chief Whip. An 'understanding' was proposed by which L R C candidates should have a clear run in a number of seats in return for support for the Liberals in others. The alternative was opposition to Liberal candidates not only in seats which the L R C would contest but elsewhere. The proposal was accepted in August 1903 and, as a result of a series of delicate negotiations – for the agreement had to remain secret – the L R C was able to look forward to straight fights in some thirty seats when the time came. For the L R C it seemed a shrewd tactical manœuvre, which made use of the movement's growing strength to gain a greater voice in Parliament while retaining freedom of action and making no commitment for the future.

In practice, it paid off handsomely. In 1900 the L R C had fixed a target of fifty Parliamentary candidates. These were either adopted and then endorsed by the L R C or agreed by trades councils and local labour representation committees after consultation with Ramsay MacDonald, who from 1904 ran the organization from an office in

Victoria Street, near Westminster. On the eve of the Election, Mac-
Donald issued a Manifesto:

> This Election is to decide whether or not Labour is to be fairly
> represented in Parliament. The House of Commons is supposed to
> be the people's House, and yet the people are not there. Landlords,
> employers, lawyers, brewers, and financiers are there in force. Why
> not Labour?

Then followed a reference to the Taff Vale case, to the neglect of old
people, crowded slums, land values, wars 'fought to make the rich
richer', unemployment and other contemporary issues. The Manifesto
ended with an appeal 'in the name of a million Trade Unionists'.

Ramsay MacDonald, first secretary of the Labour Party, with J. S. Middleton, Assistant Secretary

Free Trade and moral indignation about Chinese slave labour in South Africa were two planks of the Liberal Party's 1906 election platform

The new Labour Party   The election took place in January 1906 and resulted in a sweeping victory for the Liberal Party. But the L R C's achievement was no less: twenty-nine of its candidates were returned, twenty-two of them sponsored by the trade unions and seven by the I L P. There were, in addition, thirteen miners' M Ps, unsupported by the L R C, four other trade union members and seven further, less easily classified, 'Lib-Labs'. A total of fifty-three 'Labour men' of one sort or another compared with fifteen at the dissolution.

On 12 February 1906, the twenty-nine successful L R C candidates met together and were joined by a Durham miner who had accepted the whip, making thirty in all. They elected Keir Hardie their Chairman, and Ramsay MacDonald, who had won at Leicester, their Secretary. Three days later, the annual Conference of the L R C adopted the name 'The Labour Party'.

Keir Hardie goes canvassing in York. He was soon to be elected Chairman of the Labour Party

Rejoicing at Derby, where Richard Bell, General Secretary of the Railway Union, was re-elected

The 1906 election result was a very great advance. Even after the electoral Reform Bills of 1867 and 1884, there seemed little prospect of shaking the solid hold of the two existing parties. Generally rising standards of living and social legislation from both Conservatives and Liberals enabled them to win the working-class vote. If the Conservatives had legislated to reverse Taff Vale, and if the Liberals had declined an electoral pact but adopted many more working-class candidates of their own, the advent of an effective third party might have been postponed for many years. Their short-sightedness was Labour's opportunity and their own undoing.

What had been achieved? As it happened, the achievement of twenty years had been remarkable: no one in the mid-1880s, not even the pioneers of the SDF and Fabian Society, could have foreseen the course of events. But social change and the movement of opinion provided a climate receptive to new political ideas. The Victorian middle-classes were increasingly confronted by the ugly facts of working-class life. The university 'settlement' movement was launched by the establishment of Toynbee Hall, in the East End of London, in 1884. Evangelical Christianity gave birth to General Booth's Salvation Army and 'home missionary' activities by the Methodists. The rapid growth of public libraries in the 1890s and the beginnings of the popular press with Harmsworth's half-penny *Daily Mail* were a result of the spread of elementary education. The growth of cycling and the first steps towards the emancipation of women were further indications of fluidity in habits of mind and life. The death of Queen Victoria in 1901 signalled the brief, dazzling gaiety of Edwardian England, but the old order was changing. Even Sir William Harcourt, Gladstone's Chancellor of the Exchequer, could declare: 'We are all socialists now.'

They were not; but nor, for that matter, were most of the supporters of the Labour Representation Committee. The skill of its leaders, and especially of Keir Hardie since the formation of the ILP, had been to weld the socialism of a minority on to the self-interest of organized labour. The Labour Party in 1906 was not an avowedly socialist party. Six years earlier, at Bradford, an attempt to embrace public ownership of the means of production had been turned down. Socialism at that

Labour's twenty-nine Members of Parliament on the terrace of the House of Commons in 1906

stage would have threatened the trade union alliance. But while the rejection of SDF objectives was in this respect tactical and temporary, the rejection of class war was permanent. The Labour Party sought to bring the working class into politics and to give it Parliamentary representation, not to eliminate other classes by revolutionary action. Inevitably it relied mainly on men and women of working-class background to take the lead but it received and accepted the support of people of all classes. Already, in 1906, the Labour Party had taken on many of the characteristics that were to distinguish it from socialist movements in other countries.

57

The prospect of a Trade Disputes Bill to protect the unions intimidates the Prime Minister

Then and Now.

LIBERAL PARTY: My dear sir, I am delighted to give you a lift. It is quite a pleasure to have your company.

LIBERAL PARTY: Dear me! If he grows much bigger, I shall be crowded out of the trap altogether.

It has been resolved that the Miners' Federation shall join the Labour Party.

The Parliamentary Labour Party gained strength as trade union M P's increasingly severed their links with the Liberals

Chapter Four

AN UNEASY ALLIANCE

The new Parliament opened with a success for the Party. The doubts of the Liberals about the wisdom of legislation to reverse the Taff Vale judgment were strengthened by the Report of the Royal Commission which had been appointed in 1903. As a result, the Bill they introduced in March 1906 fell short of the trade unions' demands, in particular by leaving the unions liable for damages arising from officially authorized strike action. The Labour Party in the House of Commons, led by David Shackleton, its Vice-Chairman, then brought forward its own Bill and negotiated with the Government on points of difference. In the event, the Labour amendments were substantially accepted and the Trade Disputes Act gave the trade unions almost all for which they had asked. Trade union funds were now immune from the threat of the courts. Strikes became legal and the right to peaceful picketing was clarified. It was a considerable first victory.

The consolidation of the Parliamentary Party proceeded. Its members learnt to master procedure and to play an active part in the routine work of committees. Arthur Henderson, first as Chief Whip and then, for two years, as Chairman, brought organizing ability to the group. Friendly relations were maintained with the trade-union 'Lib-Labs' in the House and the affiliation of the Miners Federation in 1909 brought ten new members into the Parliamentary Party. In the country, much curiosity had been aroused by the sudden appearance of the Labour Party. It was followed with close interest – and very mixed sympathies – by the popular press while *The Clarion* raised its readership by half to almost 75,000.

But it proved less easy to find an effective settled role for a small minority party and to bridge the inevitable gap between Parliamentarians and impatient supporters outside. Success in 1906 had owed much to the Liberal alliance. It did again in 1910. In the General Election of December 1910, for example, twenty-seven of the forty-five Labour MPs elected won their seats in straight fights with Conservatives, three were returned unopposed and eleven in harness with a Liberal in a two-member constituency. Until 1910, the massive Liberal majority did not require them to heed seriously the voice of Labour in Parliament; more important, a heavy programme of social legislation won general approval, reducing the scope for independent action. The Workman's Compensation Act, the Trade Boards Act, the Coal Mines Act, legislation to provide school meals for needy children and to set up labour exchanges – these all represented a considerable advance. Whatever their shortcomings, the Liberals were, in any case, infinitely preferable to the Conservatives. Labour would win no credit by being the means of a change for the worse.

Liberal reform

In the country, the crucial cause of growing discontent was the failure of wages to keep up with prices. The ordinary worker became responsive to militancy of whatever kind. Inevitably, this helped further to create tension both between the leadership and the rank and file and between socialists and non-socialist trade unionists. It was predictable that Blatchford, believing propaganda more important than Parliamentary work, should be disillusioned with the Parliamentary Party and demand 'real Socialism; Socialism without dilution'. Keir Hardie replied:

Rank and file discontent: ideas and realities

> I say quite candidly that the action of the Labour Party in the House of Commons might be, and probably should be, much more strenuous than it has been; but I say with even more emphasis that no movement which is going to live to be a permanent force in the life

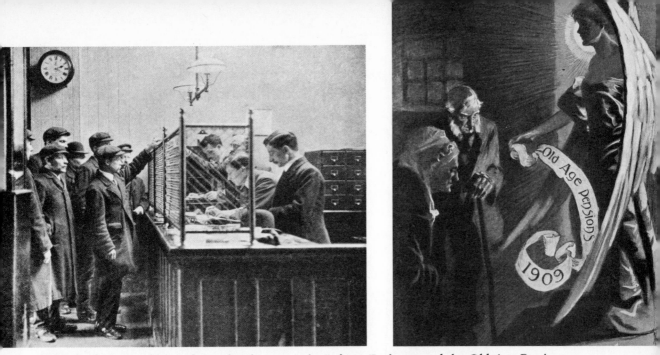

Liberal reforms in which Labour played a part – the Labour Exchange and the Old Age Pension, 'the New Year's boon to the Aged Poor'

of the nation can subsist on scenes and emotional excitements. Only in so far as a party, whether Socialist or Labour, can impress its thought and its power on the mind and will of the nation by acts of constructive statesmanship is it going to be of service in the long run.

This was a declaration which was to be repeated down the years to rank-and-file members frustrated by the absence of power and the inevitable delays and compromises of Parliamentary government. What was seen to be feasible conduct by the electorate at large appeared as a lack of militancy and drive to heavily committed supporters. Hardie also asserted the independence of the Parliamentary Party from day-to-day control from elsewhere:

> If the Party in the House is to be successful it must be free to select its own course. If the members cannot be trusted to be loyal and faithful to their great trust, then no programme and no regulations will be of any avail.

The principle was of great constitutional importance. MPs were elected by all their constituents, to whom they were ultimately responsible.

61

Victor Grayson

They could not take instructions from another body. Almost forty years later, in 1945, Clement Attlee was to reassert the independence of the Parliamentary Labour Party when the question threatened to become an election issue.

But Hardie was not proving a particularly good Parliamentary leader. In addition, illness obliged him to take a long holiday abroad which involved almost a year's absence. Victor Grayson, elected for Colne Valley in 1907 at the age of twenty-five as 'Labour and Socialist' candidate without the endorsement of either the Labour Party or the ILP, brought militancy and passion to Parliament but no sustained application. In 1908 Ben Tillett published a pamphlet called *Is the Parliamentary Party a Failure?*; and in 1910 a dissident group on the National Council of the ILP produced what came to be known as 'the Green Manifesto' (from the paper on which it was printed). *Let Us Reform the Labour Party*, which was its formal title, complained that the Parliamentary Party had 'reduced the whole Movement to acute anaemia and rabid melancholy'. At the other extreme, Beatrice Webb was noting in her diary that the 'position in the political world is most unsatisfactory'. She was disturbed at ILP attacks on Labour MPs. 'What annoys me,' she later wrote, 'is the absence of any relations, good or bad, between Labour MPs and the Labour movement in the country.' Hardie himself was worried: 'the Labour Party has ceased to count', 'the movement seems to be drifting without any settled policy.'

Beatrice Webb

Arthur Henderson

One aspect of the problem of effective amity stemmed from temperamental and policy differences between the Socialists, mainly from the ILP, and the trade unionists. The alliance forged at Bradford required nursing along. The new Party was an uneasy coalition, with little more in common amongst its supporters than a desire to see working men properly represented in Parliament. David Shackleton explained: 'the Labour Party in Parliament is essentially a practical Party. It contains within it men who have had large experience in dealing with the every-day affairs of life. . . .' But while this approach appealed to the TUC, it was hardly the language of protest that visionaries expected. Henderson, whose influence was increasing, had been an active Liberal right up to the time of his election for Barnard Castle in 1903 at the age of forty. He had called the ILP 'a national curse' and been described in turn by the SDF as 'a camp follower of the Liberal Party'. Hardie associated his Chairmanship with 'reaction and timidity'. The trade unions, on the other hand, were unhappy about the influence of the socialists, the cotton workers going so far as to seek to reduce the representation of the socialist societies on the Party executive. In 1911, there was a sharp difference of opinion on the major measure of the Parliamentary session, Lloyd George's Insurance Bill. A minority of the Party voted against it, in protest against the contributory system which the trade unions were willing to accept. In the country, the ILP shared a platform with the Fabians in opposition to it.

Lloyd George's contributory National Insurance scheme aroused mixed feelings in Labour's ranks

THE DAWN OF HOPE.

Mr. LLOYD GEORGE'S National Health Insurance Bill provides for the insurance of the Worker in case of Sickness.

Support the Liberal Government in their policy of **SOCIAL REFORM.**

H. M. Hyndman

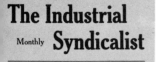

The Industrial
Monthly Syndicalist

Vol. 1. No. 1.   ONE PENNY.   July, 1910

Prepare for Action
By TOM MANN.

he Great World Movement.
In the twentieth century it is
no longer possible for members
of any political or religious
party whatever to deny that
there is, on foot, a great world
Movement aiming definitely and deter-
minedly at the economic emancipation
of the workers.

Even those, who, for obvious reasons,
regard this as the greatest evil, have
come to realise the futility of attempting
to combat this Movement by burying
their heads in the sand and pretending
to themselves that its influence is merely
local and transitory.

There is no need for us to slur over
our real weaknesses — weaknesses
which, by the way, our opponents have
without exception failed to note.

A Syndicalist journal

Within the I L P a debate went on about whether the alliance with the Labour Party – essentially with the trade unions – should continue. The rump of the S D F, after several groups had splintered off, transformed itself into the Social Democratic Party in 1907. In 1911 it was restyled again as the British Socialist Party, attracting in addition dissidents from the I L P.

The British Socialist Party – with Hyndman still prominent after thirty years of campaigning – was one of a number of symptoms of disillusionment at Parliamentary tactics and constitutional processes. The leadership of the trade unions faced growing industrial unrest and, with it, unofficial action. In the summer of 1910, Tom Mann returned as a Syndicalist from a ten-year stay in Australia, and undertook an organizing campaign amongst the dockers. The case for direct action and the use of the General Strike as a political weapon in the class war gained support. Ideas from France, anarchist in origin, and from revolutionary trade unionism in the United States, encouraged criticism both of cautious trade union leaders and orthodox trade union structure. 'Syndicalism', noted Beatrice Webb, taking time off from preparations to launch the weekly *New Statesman*, 'has taken the place of the old-fashioned Marxism. The angry youth . . . is now always a Syndicalist. . . . The inexperienced middle-class idealist has accepted with avidity the ideal of the Syndicalist as a new and exciting Utopia.' In the autumn of 1910, there was a lock-out of cotton workers in Lancashire and boiler-makers in the North-East and, in November, violence followed by the use of troops in South Wales. The following year saw a wave of national strikes – the *Daily Herald* was founded in support of one of them – starting with the seamen, spreading to dockers and transport workers, and later involving 145,000 railwaymen. But the largest strike of all was in March 1912, when 850,000 miners were brought out. Unlike the 'new unionism' of 1889, the industrial unrest of these pre-war years did not have immediate political results. But it showed a widespread and potentially dangerous discontent with existing social and political organization.

The capacity of the Labour Party to respond to this challenge was threatened by the Osborne Judgment of 1909. Osborne, a member of

A strike of miners in South Wales in November 1910 led to rioting, and troops were eventually called in. (*Right*) Wrecked shops boarded up at Tonypandy. (*Below*) The funeral of a miner killed in the disturbances

Dockers' children waiting for food during the 1912 strike

(*Right*) The new *Daily Herald*, with a Will Dyson cartoon

(*Above*) The start of the 1912 Dock strike, with Ben Tillett addressing the strikers.
(*Above right*) Police and soldiers escort a food convoy in Liverpool

(*Right*) The Labour Party in the House of Commons, 1911

The Osborne Judgment the Railway Servants and an active Liberal, believed that the unions should not become involved in political activity and objected to the use of union funds for political purposes. After a long struggle in his own union, which he eventually lost, this view was upheld by the House of Lords, on the grounds that the 1876 Act did not expressly include political action amongst the proper purposes of a trade union; and because Labour MPs who received an allowance from their union were required to abide by the decisions of the Parliamentary Party. The financial basis of the Labour Party was, as Beatrice Webb put it, 'smashed'.

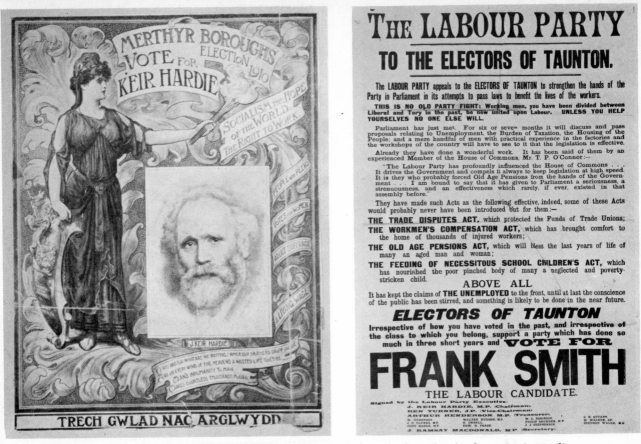

Election posters of 1910. (*Right*) Labour claims a share of the credit for Liberal reforms. Keir Hardie (*left*) bitterly attacked Liberals 'of the Churchill type'. (Churchill, then Home Secretary, had been responsible for sending troops to Wales.)

If the immediate effect on the General Election of 1910 was slight, the long-term consequences, as existing funds were exhausted and union after union became the subject of injunctions, were likely to be quite disastrous. A voluntary levy, to which members of a union would individually choose to subscribe, would clearly not achieve comparable results. Pressure on the Liberal Government led to an election promise in December 1910 to introduce payment of MPs, and the following year a financial resolution established Parliamentary salaries at the rate of £400 a year. But the trade unions wanted a clear return to the

Salaries for MPs

Suffragettes (*left*) marching off under arrest after an attack on Buckingham Palace. (*Right*) George Lansbury's supporters at the Bromley and Bow by-election, fought (and lost) in support of the suffragette movement

Mr and Mrs Lansbury

previous position, in which a levy could be imposed for whatever political purposes were agreed by the union, and in 1913 the necessary Act was passed. Political expenditure was legalized, provided only that it was from a separate political fund created after a ballot and that members could 'contract-out' of the political fund if they wished without sacrificing other membership rights. It is ironic that the Liberal Party thus provided the Labour Party with the financial means essential to political power and electoral success.

But the period from 1910 to 1914 was not otherwise a fruitful one for the Labour Party. It contested fourteen by-elections without a victory and lost four seats, one because George Lansbury resigned his seat at Bow and Bromley in order to fight the by-election as an independent in support of the suffragette movement. The party as a whole was lukewarm towards woman's suffrage and even Hardie and Philip Snowden, who had given positive support, stopped short of approving the excesses of militancy.

What, then, was the balance sheet of the first eight years of the new Labour Party? In the first place, there had been positive advances in organization and, in particular, in building up support at local level where it mattered. In 1914 there were local Labour organizations of one sort or another in 158 areas and, more important in terms of continuity and propaganda, 672 ILP branches. Strength was greatest in the North of England, in London and in Scotland. Ramsay MacDonald became Chairman of the Parliamentary Party in 1911 and the following year relinquished the secretaryship of the organization in the country to Arthur Henderson. Henderson, who had a good local Labour associa/tion in Barnard Castle, proved an able national organizer, and began to build up an effective central organization.

Secondly, on the credit side, there was being gradually established a firm body of opinion committed to the Party – whatever its faults – as the only constructive instrument for change. A 'Socialist Unity' campaign in 1913–14 failed because even the critics of the Labour Party in the ILP preferred the trade union alliance to doctrinaire

The Labour Party Executive, 1912. *Seated:* R.J. Wilson, J.Keir Hardie, J.Ramsay MacDonald, Ben Turner, W.C. Robertson, Tom Fox, George Roberts. *Standing:* J.S. Middleton, A.Peters, J.Hodge, A. Henderson, E.R. Pease, J.J. Stephenson

Marxism and the barren agitation of revolutionary socialists. Despite frustration and discontent, the political movement was sorting itself out.

No one can know the precise course which developments would have taken if the Parliament of 1910 had run its term in normal conditions. But on 28 June 1914 the Austrian Archduke Ferdinand was assassinated in the Bosnian capital of Sarajevo and five weeks later Britain declared war on Germany. Four years were to pass and ten million men were to die before peace was restored. By then the face of Britain, and her place in the world, had radically changed. For the Labour Party as for the nation, August 1914 was the end of an era.

Crowds cheering the declaration of war in 1914

Chapter Five

War presented the Labour Movement with an acute crisis of conscience. Events had moved fast since the murder of the Archduke and had taken the public by surprise. Despite imperial rivalry, naval competition, trouble in the Balkans and growing tension throughout Europe, most people believed there would be no war. The shock was greater for those in the Labour Movement for whom foreign policy was a conspiracy based on power politics and war an extension of it imposed against the popular will.

To Keir Hardie the Boer War had been 'a capitalist war' and the Labour Party's 1906 election manifesto had declared unequivocally, 'wars are fought to make the rich richer'. In its condemnation of secret diplomacy and imperialism, the Party marched in step with radical Liberals but its views were strengthened by contact with socialists abroad. In the Stuttgart declaration of 1907, the Second International, of which the Labour Party was a member, made clear that it was the duty of the working classes 'to do everything to prevent the outbreak of war by whatever means seems to them most effective'. If war nevertheless broke out, they should 'strive with all their power to make use of the violent economic and political crisis . . . to rouse the people and thereby hasten the abolition of capitalist class rule'. The enemy of socialists was not Germany but the barbarous tyranny of Czarist Russia. In 1910

71

Hardie had been greatly impressed by the tough single-mindedness of the German Social Democrats, whose Congress he attended. He proposed the use of a General Strike as a means to prevent war and in 1912 the Labour Party Conference agreed to investigate how far the threat of a stoppage of work could forestall the outbreak of hostilities. A national campaign against militarism and its consequences and a special conference on disarmament were both part of a consistent anti-war policy.

But admirable though the sentiments of the leadership were, they did not constitute a clear and constructive alternative foreign policy. There was a tendency to deny realities rather than face them. The articulate mood of the Party was resolutely pacifist on political grounds, yet a viable political solution was not sought. The exceptions amongst the leadership probably represented most accurately the views of the great majority of potential Labour voters. For years Blatchford had warned of what he believed to be German preparations for a war of conquest; and Hyndman, in his old age, was fanatically anti-German. As war approached, there was reason to doubt whether hostilities could be prevented by the solidarity of the workers, tragic though the failure and its consequences would be. An international demonstration held in Brussels at which Keir Hardie spoke, together with Jean Jaurès for France and Hugo Haase for Germany, was followed on 2 August by a great anti-war rally in Trafalgar Square. It was addressed by Hardie

Keir Hardie addresses the anti-war rally

Anti-German feeling: (*Left*) The white feather flag for pacifists, often denounced as pro-German. (*Right*) Breaking-up shops with German name-signs in the East End of London

and Henderson and resolved that the Government 'should rigidly decline to engage in war but should confine itself to efforts to bring about peace as speedily as possible'. At this stage Hardie still considered that an international strike could render war impossible: what quarrel had the British worker with his German comrade or the German with his French?

But the German invasion of Belgium and then Britain's entry into the war brought about a significant, and painful, change in attitudes. Hardie was shouted down in his own constituency and was forced to admit that once the lads had 'gone forth to fight their country's battles' they must not be disheartened by dissension at home. The Parliamentary Party, which had been against British intervention a few days before, now agreed not to oppose supplementary estimates for the war. As a result, MacDonald resigned as leader and Henderson replaced him. Labour joined the other political parties in declaring an electoral truce. The TUC for its part proposed an industrial truce in the interests of the war effort and gave its support to the army recruiting campaign.

Labour's honourable, if naïve, adherence to pacific internationalism and its belief in the capacity of workers' solidarity to save Europe from

A change of attitude

73

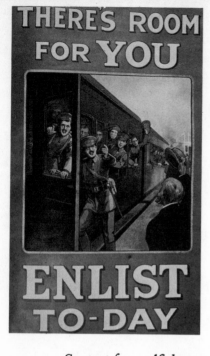

THE WAR IN EUROPE

MANIFESTO

—OF THE—

Independent Labour Party.

It has long been earnestly urged by the Independent Labour Party that the diplomatic policies pursued by European rulers, including our own, and supported by the force of murderous armaments, would lead inevitably to universal war or, universal bankruptcy—or both. That prediction, based upon facts and tendencies, has been only too swiftly and tragically fulfilled.

The Cause of the War.

Instead of striving to unite Europe in a federation of States, banded together for peace, diplomacy has deliberately aimed at dividing Europe into two armed, antagonistic camps, the Triple Entente and the Triple Alliance. Diplomacy has been underground, secret, deceitful, each Power endeavouring by wile and stratagem to get the better of its neighbour. Diplomats have breathed the very air of jealousy, deception, and distrust. Each country, in turn, largely through the influence of its Jingo Press, has been stampeded by fear and panic. Each country has tried to outstrip other countries in the vastness and costliness of its war machine. Powerful armament interests have played their sinister part, for it is they who reap rich harvest out of havoc and death. When all this has been done, any spark will start a conflagration like the present.

It is difficult and perhaps futile to try to apportion at this moment the exact measure of responsibility and blame which the various countries must bear. It is just as untrue to say that British policy has been wholly white and German policy wholly black as to say that German policy has been entirely right and British policy entirely wrong. Simple undiscriminating people in both countries may accept unreservedly one or other of these alternatives, but, as past experience shows, history will tell a different story.

Secret Diplomacy.

For the present Sir Edward Grey issues his White Paper to prove Germany the aggressor, just as Germany issues a White Paper to prove Russia the aggressor, and Russia to prove Austria the aggressor. Even if every word in the British White Paper be admitted, the wider indictment remains. Let it be acknowledged that in the days immediately preceding the war, Sir Edward Grey worked for peace. It was too late. Over a number of years, together with other diplomats, he had himself dug the abyss, and wise statesmanship would have foreseen, and avoided, the certain result.

It was not the Servian question or the Belgian question that pulled this country into the deadly struggle. Great Britain is not at war because of oppressed nationalities or Belgian neutrality. Even had Belgian neutrality not been wrongfully infringed by Germany we should still have been drawn in.

If France in defiance of treaty rights had invaded Belgium to get at Germany, who believes we should have begun hostilities against France? Behind the back of Parliament and people, the British Foreign Office gave secret understandings to France, denying their existence when challenged. That is why this country is now face to face with the red ruin and impoverishment of war. Treaties and agreements have dragged Republican France at the heels of despotic Russia, Britain at the heels of France. At the proper time all this will be made plain, and the men responsible called to account. [P.T.O.

(Far left) Recruiting poster. *(Left)* The ILP Manifesto denounces interests on both sides as responsible for the war

---

Support for the war

self-destruction had been shattered by the impact of war. As 1914 ended, the position of the bulk of the Labour Movement, especially the moderate centre of trade unionists and including most Fabians, was that they supported the war, which they assumed would be short. But they did not approve a war of conquest. They also wanted a clear statement of allied war aims. Naturally there were exceptions to this general consensus and differences of emphasis within it. Even families were divided: Clement Attlee, who was doing social work and becoming politically active in the East End, joined the army and ended the war in hospital; his brother became a conscientious objector and ended the war in jail. Some Labour spokesmen, such as Blatchford and Hyndman, were extremely belligerent and nationalistic. Others, including a large section of the ILP and a majority of the British Socialist Party, remained opposed to the war throughout its course. They were frequently denounced as 'pro-German', but this was unfair. They saw the outbreak of hostilities as a tragedy, the responsibility for which was widely spread. Their attachment to internationalism did not waver. 'Across the roar of guns,' proclaimed an ILP manifesto, a week after the declaration of war, 'we send sympathy and greeting to the German Socialists. . . . They are no enemies of ours but faithful friends.' They

74

Lloyd George's Imperial War Cabinet, 1917. Henderson is second from the right

found some sympathizers among radical liberals who often joined them in forming active pacifist organizations; the best known, the Union of Democratic Control, had MacDonald, Snowden and Trevelyan among its officers. Trevelyan, like many Liberal pacifists, was later brought by his opposition to the war to join the Labour Party.

Differences about the war did not destroy the Labour Party because its loose federal structure and the absence of a central dogma allowed a broad range of opinions to persist within it and above all because Henderson and the majority leaders did not attempt to discipline or expel the minority. But they did make it difficult for the Party in the House of Commons to function as a united body. This was illustrated in May 1915 when Asquith offered Labour a share in his reconstructed Coalition. Several in the Parliamentary Party, including MacDonald, Snowden and Clynes, were against acceptance. When the majority vote was for participation, and Henderson joined the Cabinet as President of the Board of Education, they moved to sit on the opposition benches in the Commons. The question came up again at the end of 1916 when Asquith was driven from power and Lloyd George, the new Prime Minister, invited Labour to join him. MacDonald, Snowden and the left wing remained irreconcilably opposed but

Labour joins the Coalition

75

Henderson persuaded the Party to join, despite its dislike of the way in which Lloyd George had forced his way to power. Henderson went into the new small War Cabinet. John Hodge was made Minister of Labour and G. W. Barnes of the Engineers became Minister of Pensions. Both decisions to participate in the Government, in 1915 and in 1916, were subsequently approved by large Conference majorities.

By 1916 it seemed that the anti-war socialists were defeated. In Parliament they were opposed by a majority of their own Party. In the country they appeared lone voices during the first two years of the war. Then unexpectedly there occurred a swing of opinion in their direction. Several factors influenced this change within the Party. People became weary of the war, recoiling from the horrors of the Somme, where 60,000 Britons died in a day without seeming to improve the prospects of victory. Even the trade unions, hitherto most firm in their support of the war, began to feel that working people were carrying more than their

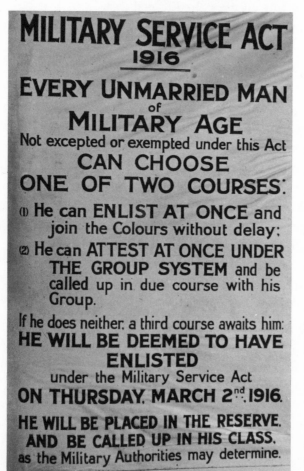

Recruitment posters. Despite Labour opposition, by 1916 the Government was introducing compulsory conscription by stages

A Labour Party delegation to Russia, April 1917: Will Thorne, J. O'Grady, William Saunders. The Russian soldiers belong to the first regiment to declare for the revolution by refusing to fire upon the people

fair share of the nation's sacrifices, and they opposed the introduction of conscription.

In this atmosphere of growing dissatisfaction the Labour Movement received the exhilarating news of the Russian Revolution and the overthrow of the hated Czar in March 1917. In May the new Russian Government under the social democrat Kerensky proposed a Conference in Stockholm to discuss War Aims. Arthur Henderson was immediately sent to Russia to report back to the British Government on the situation there. He became convinced that Russia could not continue the war, and that Britain should support the Stockholm Conference as an instrument for fostering peace. But Henderson returned to find that the Cabinet was hostile to the Stockholm venture and Lloyd George had withdrawn support. Properly indignant, he resigned in August. His resignation did not bring Labour out of the Coalition – formal support continued and G. W. Barnes took Henderson's place in the War Cabinet. Nor, in the event, did the Stockholm Conference ever take place. Yet Labour's mood changed rapidly towards the end of 1917. With Henderson now leading the anti-Government group, the I L P and trade union wings of the movement were brought much closer to a common desire for peace and a common awareness that they could put little faith in Lloyd George. The Bolshevik Revolution late

The Russian Revolution

in 1917 was rapidly followed by the announcement of peace negotiations between Russia and Germany. Early in December, President Wilson delivered to the United States Congress the first of his famous messages on War Aims. Talk of an end to war was in the air. On 28 December a Labour Conference in London approved a revised Memorandum on War Aims. Henderson was the driving force behind this, working to unite the Labour Party in Britain and the allied socialist parties in support of a negotiated peace without territorial annexations. The Memorandum also urged that the peace treaty should provide for a 'Super-National Authority, or League of Nations'.

Labour now had a separate, internationalist and peace-seeking foreign policy. At the same time, work was afoot to reform the Party's constitution, its organization and its policy objectives. The chief agents of this reconstruction were Henderson and Sidney Webb, two very different personalities representing different sections of the Party. Henderson was a practical man whose roots were firmly planted in the trade unions. But by 1917, when he resigned the Party leadership to devote his energies to reforming the Party, he appreciated that a national party must have a coherent and unifying faith. Evolutionary socialism of the Fabian brand appealed most to him. This led him to Sidney Webb, who by 1916 was the Fabian member of the Party Executive. Henderson harnessed his own and Webb's divergent talents and directed them towards transforming the Labour Party.

The first step in this direction was the new Party constitution, drafted by Webb and Henderson in 1917 and adopted by a Party Conference in February 1918. Previously Labour's sole stated objective was 'to organize and maintain in Parliament and in the country a political Labour Party'. It was hardly an inspiring aim, but it was limited by political necessity. For up to 1914 any attempt to define the Party's objectives would have produced a damaging clash between those who wanted a commitment to socialism and the majority of trade unionists who were indifferent or hostile to doctrine. War had weakened this opposition to socialism and the new draft constitution was able to introduce a vision of a socialist society. It set out the object of the Party as being: '. . . to secure for the producers by hand and by brain the full

Arthur Henderson addresses the Labour Party's War Aims Conference

fruits of their industry and the most equitable distribution thereof that may be possible upon the basis of the common ownership of the means of production and the best obtainable system of popular administration and control of each industry and service'.

As a number of prominent Liberals and intellectuals had been attracted to Labour by socialist efforts to bring about peace, it followed that membership of the Party ought to be opened up. Hitherto the only means of entry for non-manual workers was through one of the socialist societies. Yet their combined membership was no more than 75,000 in 1918. They were clearly unsuitable as instruments for the kind of mass recruitment Labour needed, especially among the six million women just about to get the vote. Consequently a new national Party organiza-tion was established, and added to the existing federation of trade unions and socialist societies. It aimed to set up a local Labour party in every Parliamentary constituency to recruit individuals 'who subscribe to the constitution and programme of the Party'. Five of the twenty-three members of the reconstituted National Executive Committee were to represent these local Labour parties. Four other places were reserved for women.

New Party organization

Having re-written the constitution and reconstructed the Party organization it was now necessary to draw up a full programme of policies which would appeal to the enlarged post-war electorate (twenty-one and a quarter million compared to seven and three-quarter million in 1910) and present Labour as a potential Government. This was done in a remarkable and historic document, *Labour and the New Social Order*, mainly drafted by Sidney Webb and approved by the 1918 Party Conference. It begins by stating firmly the need to build 'a new social order based, not on internecine conflict, inequality of riches and dominion over subject classes . . . but on the deliberately planned co-operation in production and distribution . . . the widest possible participation in power, both economic and political, and the general consciousness of concert which characterizes a true democracy'. It goes on to set out a detailed programme for public ownership of land and certain basic industries, central planning of the economy, the maintenance of full employment and the provision of adequate welfare and social security. These were to constitute the core of the Party's domestic programmes for the next quarter of a century and of the actual policy which Labour carried out after 1945. In the more immediate future this 'reconstruction manifesto' also provided British democratic socialists with a firm base of policy and faith from which to resist the revolutionary blandishments of the 'Communist Manifesto', which was to appear from the First Congress of the Third International nine months later in March 1919.

In the autumn of 1918 political upheavals in Germany, following upon the allied breakthrough on the Western front, improved the prospect of a swift conclusion to the war. On 9 November the Kaiser abdicated. A German Republic was proclaimed and on the eleventh the Armistice was signed.

A special Party Conference was immediately summoned, and the Executive put down a resolution urging that Labour should withdraw its membership from the Coalition at the close of the present Parliament. It was opposed by most of the Parliamentary Labour Party and a few unions, partly on the grounds that Labour should retain its place in the Coalition in order to have a say in making the peace,

Women munitions workers. Women over thirty were rewarded with the right to vote when the war ended

and that to oppose Lloyd George was to court disaster at the coming election. But the majority of delegates shared the Executive's view and the Labour Ministers, with four exceptions, resigned from office and moved into Opposition.

Superficially the stresses of war had at first threatened great damage to the Labour Party. Both its leaders and its rank and file had been divided. Yet in the long run war proved to be a dynamic and unifying influence. By the Armistice Labour had successfully negotiated its institutional transition from a minority pressure group to a national party capable of governing the nation. Its membership, reflecting the great war-time expansion in the trade union movement, had doubled since 1913 to three million. It had defined its principles and declared its policy objectives. It had established a nation-wide organization open to membership of all classes. It had proclaimed its freedom for political action independent of the older parties. There were other features of the heritage from 1914-18 which were conducive to Labour's subsequent progress. War had shown the country's total dependence in emergency

The effects of the war

81

Mr Lloyd George: '. . . every patriotic woman should support those who won the war.'
Mrs Atkins: 'Then why didn't you put off the election till the men come home and give
'em a chance of voting?'

upon the common people of Britain. It had led to those people – or at
least all men over twenty-one and women over thirty – receiving the
vote by the 1918 Representation of the People's Act. It had demonstrated
the viability and value of state activity in the economy and in particular
industries. It had allowed some Labour leaders to gain experience in
the highest councils of state and the Party to act in public for the first
time completely separately from the Liberals. It had left the two older
parties with the stigma and blame for the horrors of the Western front.
Labour, which down to 1916 had been vilified for the 'unpatriotic'
pacifism of some of its supporters, ultimately stood to benefit from the
public weariness of war and disillusionment with the peace settlements.

*The 1918
'Coupon
Election'*
But the fruits of these years, and especially of Henderson's and
Webb's labours, were not yet to be harvested. In the 1918 'Coupon
Election', which Lloyd George rushed in the euphoric wake of the
Armistice, exploiting emotive slogans such as 'Hang the Kaiser' and
'make Germany pay till the pips squeak', the Coalition enjoyed a land-
slide victory and Labour appeared to suffer seriously. Although the

Party had greatly expanded its number of candidates – 363 were endorsed – representation in the Commons rose only to fifty-seven compared with forty-five in 1910. Forty-nine of those elected were trade unionists, twenty-five from the Miners' Federation alone. Only three of fifty ILP candidates and five out of 140 local Labour Party candidates were successful. Among the casualties were many of the Party's best known leaders. Arthur Henderson, Ramsay MacDonald, Snowden, F. W. Jowett and George Lansbury all went down heavily. Ernest Bevin, Walter Citrine and Sidney Webb, later to make lasting names in the movement, were among defeated newcomers to the hustings. Yet in retrospect it can be seen that the result was not as discouraging as it first appeared. Labour had received two and a quarter million of the eleven million votes cast: compared with 1910 it had trebled its share of the total poll to 24 per cent. This was not a bad popular base. Moreover it was fighting for the first time as a separate Party without the help of the Liberal alliance – and still it increased its number of MPs. In the long run this proof that it could win independent of election pacts was of great significance. But in its bid for the highest stakes of power the Party still had a hard road ahead.

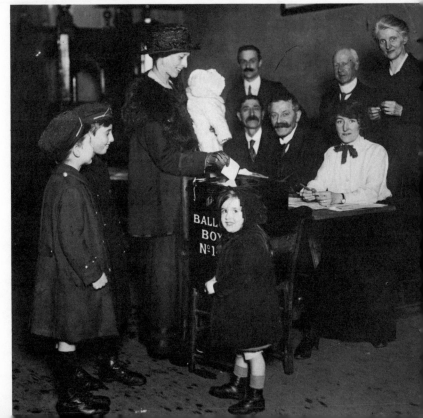

The 1918 election: women vote for the first time

The Labour team returned to Parliament in late 1918 was weak and offered little hope of speedily advancing the movement's political cause. The trade unions, on the other hand, were temporarily in a strong bargaining position and concentrated their immediate efforts on industry while the brief post-war boom lasted. But from 1920 the economy began to slide into recession. Certain harsh economic realities had to be faced once the surge of domestic demand, pent-up by war, had exhausted itself. Britain had emerged victorious in 1918 but with her industrial supremacy much reduced. Severe competition faced all the products basic to her economy – especially coal, steel and textiles. British businessmen, hard-faced men who had undoubtedly done well out of the war, were incapable of adjusting to the new challenge of peace. Their only response to competition was to force down the wages of their workers. The index of real wages fell from 111 in 1921 to ninety-seven in 1922 and to ninety-five in 1923. Unemployment rose dramatically. Only 2·5 per cent in 1920, it was never below 11 per cent in 1921–3. Out-of-work veterans appeared in the streets singing for pennies. Lloyd George's Government made things worse by accelerating the 'return to normalcy', halting the post-war housing drive to build 'homes for heroes' and cutting expenditure on social services. In September 1921 the Mayor of Poplar and twenty-nine councillors were

85

◀ (*Left*) Unemployment distress in Lancashire, 1923

A queue of unemployed outside a Labour Exchange

(*Above right*) Demonstrators marching to the High Court in support of the prosecuted ▶
Mayor and Councillors of Poplar, London, in 1921

imprisoned because the borough, burdened with expenditure on unemployment relief, would not pay the sums due to the LCC for local government purposes.

The effect of these developments, together with the collapse of the Triple Alliance in support of the miner's strike on 'Black Friday', 1921, was to divert Labour's energies back from industrial to political action and hopes centred increasingly on a General Election victory. Moreover, to an increasing number of people among the middle as well as the working class, Labour's programme appeared less and less a utopian doctrine, more and more the only practical remedy to the terrible economic plight of Britain. Events at Versailles and the long wrangles over reparations added to the climate of public disillusionment. 'After four years of active service,' wrote Clement Attlee, then Mayor of Stepney, 'I have seen every ideal I fought for betrayed in the Paris Peace Conference.' The underlying idealism and morality of Labour's approach to politics naturally attracted those who were repelled by the prevailing cynicism in Government circles.

(*Right*) Clement Attlee, Mayor of Stepney (on the right), and other London Mayors join ▶
in an unemployment demonstration in 1920

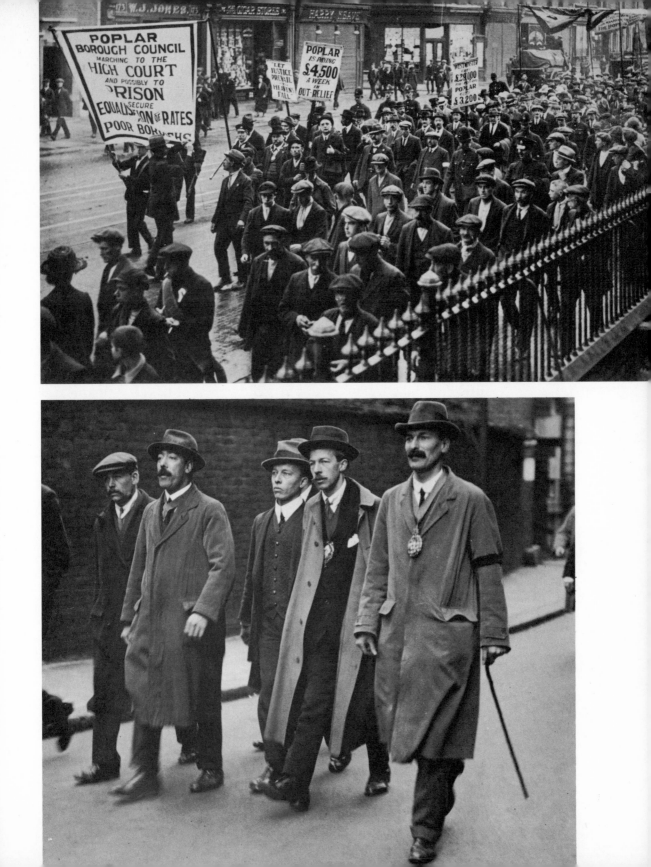

The 1922 election The first real chance to test Labour's post-war progress at the polls came in late 1922. Lloyd George, having served the Tories' purpose and shattered his own Liberal Party in the process, was manœuvred from power forever and the Conservatives won the subsequent election. But Labour, now fighting over two-thirds of all the constituencies and benefiting from the disarray of the Liberals, who were divided between the supporters of Lloyd George and of Asquith, more than doubled its number of seats to 142. Its vote rose to four and a quarter million – almost one-third of the poll. All the Party's leaders were returned, with the sadly ironic exception of Henderson, the architect of Labour's post-war growth. Among the outstanding newcomers to Parliament were Clement Attlee, Sidney Webb, Arthur Greenwood and a militant group of left-wing Clydesiders of whom James Maxton, Emanuel Shinwell and David Kirkwood were the most prominent. The new Parliamentary Party, which was officially recognized as His Majesty's Opposition, took an immediate decision on its leadership. Shinwell, on behalf of the Clydesiders and backed by most of the I L P, nominated Ramsay MacDonald, assuming from his wartime record that he was a natural left-winger. The handsome and eloquent Scot, who had vacated the leadership eight years earlier and entered the political wilderness, beat the previous leader, J. R. Clynes, by 61–56. A margin of five votes had decided who would be Labour's Prime Minister twice within the next seven years.

At Easton Lodge, the home of the Countess of Warwick, a former friend of King Edward VII. The house was often the scene of Labour Conferences. Lady Warwick extending hospitality to distinguished Labour leaders: Henderson on her right, Ramsay MacDonald on her left, and Emanuel Shinwell and his wife immediately behind

In Parliament the Party continued to gain in prestige and confidence under MacDonald's and Snowden's vigorous leadership. In the country Henderson and the national agent, Egerton Wake, rapidly built up the local organizations and women's sections throughout the country along the lines laid down in 1918. The *Daily Herald*, the only left-wing daily, was salvaged financially so that the Party and the T U C now had a reliable voice for official views – while the I L P *New Leader*, brilliantly edited by H. N. Brailsford, acted as a focus for less orthodox left-wing opinions.

By November 1923 Labour politicians were once more back on the hustings, campaigning for free trade, strengthening the League of Nations, revising the Versailles Treaty and resuming full relations with

(*Top left*) The *Daily Herald* offices with Clifford Allen, the editor, and his staff. (*Top right*) Philip Snowden. (*Right*) Ramsay MacDonald in his second period as Leader of the Labour Party

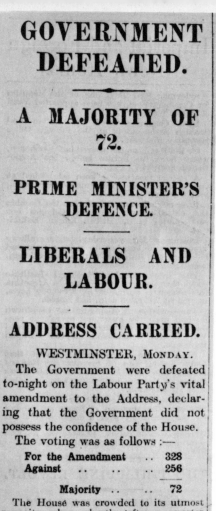

GOVERNMENT DEFEATED.

A MAJORITY OF 72.

PRIME MINISTER'S DEFENCE.

LIBERALS AND LABOUR.

ADDRESS CARRIED.

WESTMINSTER, MONDAY.

The Government were defeated to-night on the Labour Party's vital amendment to the Address, declaring that the Government did not possess the confidence of the House.

The voting was as follows :—

For the Amendment	328
Against	256
Majority	72

The House was crowded to its utmost capacity when, shortly after a quarter past 11, the result of the division was declared. There was a great burst of cheering from the Opposition benches when it was seen that Mr. Ben Spoor and Mr. F. Hall took their position to the left of the Speaker, Mr. Eyres-Monsell and Colonel Gibbs taking the position which indicated defeat. The Clerk handed the paper upon which the fateful result was inscribed to MR. SPOOR, and in a quiet voice he read out the figures.

THE LAST STAGES.

The latter stages of the debate had been followed with the keenest interest by the House and by a host of distinguished strangers. The Prince of Wales occupied the seat above the clock, being accompanied by the Duke of York, next to whom sat Lord Londonderry. The Archbishop of Canterbury sat behind the Prince and exchanged remarks with him from time to time. In the Diplomatic Gallery were the Ambassadors of France, America, Germany, and other representatives of foreign Powers. In the Imperial Gallery Mr. Stanley Bruce, Prime Minister of Australia, who was accompanied by Sir Joseph Cook, took great interest in the drama on the floor below. Mrs. Stanley Baldwin watched the scene from the Speaker's Gallery.

Russia. One issue predominated, however: work. Labour's *Manifesto* insisted that 'The Labour Party alone has a remedy for unemployment'. MacDonald bewitched a rally of supporters with the vision of the New Jerusalem ahead: '. . . we are going to make the land blossom like a rose and contain houses and firesides where there shall be happiness and contentment and glorious aspirations'. Yet few, even under MacDonald's spell, expected that Labour's roses were to have the chance to blossom forthwith. Most of the press believed that the Conservatives would be returned; some speculated that the Liberals, fighting this time as a united party, might replace Labour as the official Opposition. As it turned out the Conservatives plummeted from 346 to 259. Labour rose from 144 to 191 and the Liberals from 117 to 159. Among the transfusion of new blood to the Parliamentary Labour Party was Herbert Morrison, the able Secretary of the London Labour Party.

The result produced an unparalleled equilibrium between the three great parties. It rested with the Liberals either to keep the Tories in or to turn them out and let Labour form a minority Government. They chose to support a Labour motion of censure and on 22 January 1924 George V sent for Ramsay MacDonald to form the first Labour Government.

Several Labour leaders trembled at the consequences of their success. Sidney Webb reported to Beatrice that 'they have all, except Henderson, cold feet at the thought of office, though all of them believe J.R.M. ought not to refuse'. MacDonald did not refuse. 'For the first time in her history,' the *English Review* proclaimed, 'the party of revolution approach their hands to the helm of state, not only, as in the seventeenth century, for the purpose of overthrowing the Crown or of altering the Constitution, but with the design of destroying the very basis of civilized

The Times description of the overthrow of Baldwin's Government on a Commons vote of confidence on 21 January 1924

Formation of the first Labour Government: Ramsay MacDonald, J.H. Thomas, Arthur Henderson and J.R. Clynes outside Buckingham Palace

The first Labour Cabinet, 1924. *Seated:* W. Adamson, Lord Parmoor, P. Snowden, Lord Haldane, Ramsay MacDonald, J.R. Clynes, J.H. Thomas, Arthur Henderson. *Standing:* C.P. Trevelyan, Stephen Walsh, Lord Thomson, Lord Chelmsford, Sidney Webb, Lord Olivier, J. Wheatley, Noel Buxton, F.W. Jowett, Joshua Wedgewood, Vernon Hartshorn, Tom Shaw

life.' Neither the aspirations nor the achievements of the first Labour Government lived up to that expectation. The Cabinet erred towards respectability rather than revolution. MacDonald himself was both Prime Minister and Foreign Secretary. Snowden went to the Exchequer, Henderson to the Home Office, Sidney Webb to the Board of Trade, J. H. Thomas to the Colonial Office and Clynes was made Lord Privy Seal and Deputy Leader of the House. An ex-Liberal, Lord Haldane, was Lord Chancellor and an ex-Tory, Lord Parmoor, was Lord President of the Council. In a Cabinet of twenty, there were seven trade unionists.

But what could a minority Government achieve? Some – mainly centred in the ILP and on the Clyde – urged MacDonald to 'live dangerously' and to press on full steam ahead towards a socialist Britain. The Parliamentary leadership took a more realistic approach, in view of their dependence on the Liberals, and saw office as an opportunity to carry out useful social reform at home and to promote international co-operation abroad.

The new Government dealt first with unemployment. Benefits were improved and Snowden announced plans for road and railway construction to provide jobs. In the housing field, John Wheatley, the Minister of Health, legislated to provide subsidies to local authorities which built houses for controlled rents. Some admirable reforms were also initiated in the educational field by Charles Trevelyan. No attempt was made to enact any of the more specifically socialist parts of Labour's domestic programme. This was mainly because of the Parliamentary situation and the shortage of time, but it may also reflect the Prime Minister's concern with the international scene, in which he helped create an improved atmosphere. He persuaded the French to evacuate the Ruhr, he promoted the Dawes plan for reduced German reparations and he worked for international arbitration and disarmament through the Geneva Protocol. Labour also extended full diplomatic recognition to the Soviet Government, though MacDonald seemed less enthusiastic about this project. Two treaties of friendship were drafted and a British loan to the Soviet Union envisaged. But the press and the Conservatives waged a vitriolic campaign under the slogan 'no money for murderers',

Three Clydesiders, James Maxton, David Kirkwood and George Buchanan, arrive at Westminster for the opening of Parliament

Philip Snowden arriving at Downing Street to begin his first period as Chancellor of the Exchequer

The Prime Minister, Ramsay MacDonald, with J.H. Thomas on his right, is cheered as Parliament reassembles briefly in September 1924

A Tory 'Red Bogey' election poster; 1924, showing MacDonald welcoming the Russians and rejecting the Empire

and before the year was out Labour was to pay dearly for its efforts to improve Anglo-Russian relations.

The Government fell in a sad fashion, unworthy of even the limited promise it had shown during the previous eight months of a difficult session. The Attorney-General, Sir Patrick Hastings, had first initiated and then stopped proceedings for sedition against the editor of a Communist journal. Liberals and Tories joined in demanding a Parliamentary inquiry and the Government was heavily defeated.

The ensuing election was dominated by the fantastic affair of the 'Zinoviev Letter', copies of which were published during the campaign. This letter, which was alleged to have been sent from the Communist International to the British Communist Party, urged not only every endeavour to ensure ratification of the Anglo-Soviet treaties but also full preparation for a military insurrection in Britain. Labour candidates were put in a terrible quandary, since the Russian treaties were an important plank in the Party's platform. Curiously, MacDonald failed

94

to grasp the electoral significance of the episode and took no counter measures.

Whether the letter was authentic or not, whether or not there was, as many believed, a plot between the Tories, the press and some Foreign Office officials, Labour's political opponents exploited the situation disgracefully, inflating public hysteria over the 'Red Bogey'. On polling day Labour had a net loss of forty seats – including Morrison and Shinwell – mainly because of local Liberal-Tory alliances. There were consolations, however. The first Labour Government, despite the shortness of its term and its miserable ending, had to its credit some respectable achievements in domestic and foreign affairs. It had proved that Labour could govern responsibly. It had firmly and finally established its claim to be the only serious alternative to Conservatism – for the Liberals dropped catastrophically from 158 to 42 seats and were to remain from then onwards a smallish third party. In fact even in the defeat of 1924 Labour raised its popular vote by over a million to five and a half million. But the immediate outlook was bleak. Behind the Tories by 250 seats, and with a treasury bankrupted by three successive elections, the Party faced the prospect of long and fruitless years of Opposition again. Moreover, its leader was already the object of distrust among certain sections of Labour opinion. Beatrice Webb wrote of him in her journal as early as March 1924: 'I do not accuse him of treachery, for he was never a socialist . . . where he has lacked integrity is in *posing* as a socialist and occasionally using revolutionary jargon.' There was even an unsuccessful move to replace him as leader in the new Parliament after the election. MacDonald, for his own part,

Two Labour Party posters for the 1924 election

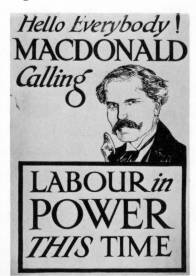

The Government publicizes its point of view about wages and costs in the coal mines in 1920 – a preview of trouble which was to lead to the 1926 General Strike

showed signs of feeling estranged from the Party, which he believed was over-critical of all he did.

While the political wing of the Labour Movement smarted from its 1924 election defeat, attention switched increasingly to the industrial scene.

Unemployment was high, around twelve per cent in 1925 and 1926. World trading conditions continued severely competitive, leading to pressure for cuts in wages. The coal industry, most exposed to international competition and with the worst owners in Britain, was predictably destined to be the main industrial battlefield. Trouble loomed there in 1925; but the TUC threatened to call a general strike and the Government took fright and offered a subsidy to end the existing lock-out while a Royal Commission, chaired by Sir Herbert Samuel, investigated the industry. The unions were jubilant and some believed that in the general strike they had an invincible weapon. 'I don't care a hang for any Government or army or navy', A. J. Cook of the Miners' Federation told a meeting, 'we have already beaten not only the employers but the strongest Government of modern times.' Cook, along with the coal owners, was equally adamant in rejecting the recommendations of the Coal Commission in 1926 and on 1 May all the pits stopped.

A. J. Cook

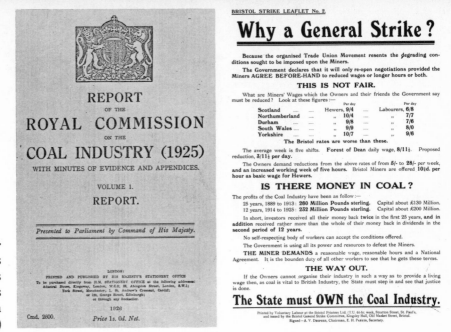

REPORT
OF THE
ROYAL COMMISSION
ON THE
COAL INDUSTRY (1925)
WITH MINUTES OF EVIDENCE AND APPENDICES.

VOLUME 1.
REPORT.

Presented to Parliament by Command of His Majesty.

LONDON:
PRINTED AND PUBLISHED BY HIS MAJESTY'S STATIONERY OFFICE
To be purchased directly from H.M. STATIONERY OFFICE at the following addresses:
Adastral House, Kingsway, London, W.C.2; 28, Abingdon Street, London, S.W.1;
York Street, Manchester; 1, St. Andrew's Crescent, Cardiff;
or 120, George Street, Edinburgh;
or through any Bookseller.

1926

Cmd. 2600.   *Price 1s. 0d. Net.*

BRISTOL STRIKE LEAFLET No. 2.

Why a General Strike?

Because the organised Trade Union Movement resents the degrading conditions sought to be imposed upon the Miners.

The Government declares that it will only re-open negotiations provided the Miners AGREE BEFORE-HAND to reduced wages or longer hours or both.

THIS IS NOT FAIR.

What are Miners' Wages which the Owners and their friends the Government say must be reduced? Look at these figures:—

		Per day		Per day
Scotland	....	Hewers, 9/4	.... Labourers,	6/8
Northumberland	....	„ 10/4	.... „	7/7
Durham	....	„ 9/8	.... „	7/6
South Wales	....	„ 9/9	.... „	8/0
Yorkshire	....	„ 10/7	.... „	9/6

The Bristol rates are worse than these.

The average week is five shifts. **Forest of Dean** daily wage, **8/11½.** Proposed reduction, 3/11½ per day.

The Owners demand reductions from the above rates of from **5/-** to **28/-** per week, and an increased working week of five hours. Bristol Miners are offered **10½d.** per hour as basic wage for Hewers.

IS THERE MONEY IN COAL?

The profits of the Coal Industry have been as follow:—

25 years, 1889 to 1913 : **260 Million Pounds sterling.** Capital about £130 Million.
12 years, 1914 to 1925 : **252 Million Pounds sterling.** Capital about £200 Million.

In short, investors received all their money back **twice** in the first 25 years, **and in addition** received rather more than the whole of their money back in dividends in the second period of 12 years.

No self-respecting body of workers can accept the conditions offered.

The Government is using all its power and resources to defeat the Miners.

THE MINER DEMANDS a reasonable wage, reasonable hours and a National Agreement. It is the bounden duty of all other workers to see that he gets these terms.

THE WAY OUT.

If the Owners cannot organise their industry in such a way as to provide a living wage then, as coal is vital to British Industry, the State must step in and see that justice is done.

The State must OWN the Coal Industry.

Printed by Voluntary Labour at the Bristol Printers Ltd. (T.U. 44-hr. week, Stratton Street, St. Paul's, and issued by the Bristol General Strike Committee, Kingsley Hall, Old Market Street, Bristol.
Signed—A. V. Despres, Chairman, E. H. Parker, Secretary.

The Samuel Royal Commission's recommendations were rejected by both unions and employers. The miners demanded nationalization in their strike leaflet (*far right*)

The General Strike

Once again the TUC took over the negotiations with the Government in expectation that under the threat of a general strike the Government would again climb down. But Churchill and others in the Cabinet, having now made preparations to maintain essential services in case of a strike, wanted a fight. They broke off negotiations and the TUC was left with no alternative other than to call out its members. Some unionists enjoyed the prospect of a titanic struggle with their country's government. A minority of Marxists and Syndicalists, who had considerable influence in these early post-war years, believed they could revolutionize society by industrial warfare. A much larger group, personified by Cook, shared in the windy talk of revolution though they had never seriously prepared for it. These bogus revolutionaries bear much of the responsibility for the tragic outcome of 1926, for they whipped up a large following among the mass of workers without having any clear idea of where and how to lead it. Most British trade unionists, however, were undoubtedly moderate, even conservative, and they joined out of loyalty to the miners, not to overthrow the state. Prominent among them were Walter Citrine and Ernest Bevin, who were elected to key union posts in October 1925, one as TUC General Secretary and the other as a member of the General Council. They were

97

Strikers at London's East India Dock

to dominate the movement throughout the rest of the inter-war period; but during the vital days of the strike it was fatally unclear which of the different voices among the unions was supposed to hold command.

On 3 May the first phase of the strike began, with the transport, iron and steel, building and printing industries brought to a standstill. The solidarity of the workers' response to the strike call was astonishing. Altogether during the nine days that it lasted, one and a half million men downed tools to support the million miners already locked out. Of 30,000 train crews on the LMS railway, only 400 reported to work on the first day of the strike. That day not a single bus moved in London. No cargoes were unloaded in London docks until volunteers were brought in under the protection of troops with machine guns and armoured cars. In the provinces every pit, every steel works, every iron furnace was still. Although there was no serious bloodshed, occasional violence broke out and the police charged crowds of strikers in several towns. The strikers and their families remained in surprisingly good humour and the sense of solidarity and comradeship between the men produced a feeling of communal exhilaration. The local strike committees organized entertainments and meetings and provided meals for the most needy. At Plymouth the strikers played the police at football and won 3–1.

But the strike did not succeed in paralysing the country. Many volunteers streamed to join Churchill's Organization for the Maintenance of Supplies, providing emergency transport services and working in the docks. With their help essential services were maintained and the

Mounted police
clear rioters at the
Elephant and
Castle, London

Armoured cars es-
cort a food convoy
through Hyde
Park

Volunteer bus
driver with police
escort in Central
London

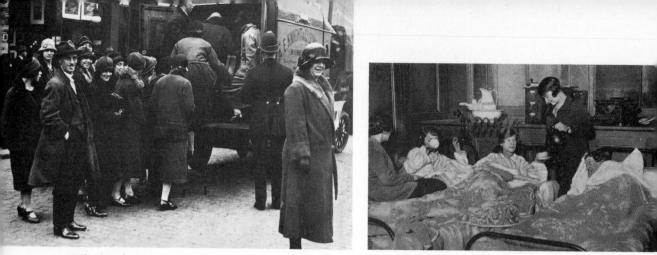

Office workers
beating the strike

Sir Herbert Samuel

impact of the strike softened. The weather held fine and stocks of fuel lasted.

The Government flatly refused to negotiate with the strike leaders: '. . . there can be no question of compromise of any kind,' declared the *British Gazette*, the Government's newspaper. 'Either the country will break the General Strike, or the General Strike will break the country.'

Rumours were current that the Government intended to arrest members of the General Council, to impound union funds and to call up the army reservists. The General Council for its part maintained a firm public face and ordered the second phase of the campaign on 11 May: the engineers and the shipworkers were called out.

But behind the scenes the realists in the TUC were looking urgently for a compromise which would enable its members to go back to work and earn their living without sacrificing the honour and interests of the miners. Sir Herbert Samuel issued a Memorandum, proposing the renewal of the Government's subsidy to the coal industry, the resumption of negotiations between owners and unions, and no revision of wages until the reorganization of the industry was set in train. The General Council, assuming that the Memorandum had the Government's approval, accepted it as a basis for re-opening negotiations. But the miners' leaders argued that they had no guarantee that the Government or the owners would accept the Memorandum – and anyway it assumed an eventual reduction in wages, to which they could never agree. They were prepared to sit out the strike indefinitely and insisted that it was for them finally to decide on what terms their members should return to work. But the other unions had joined in to produce a settlement, not to participate in a seemingly endless and financially ruinous war of attrition. They felt that they also should have an important voice in determining the terms on which the strike would be ended – and that the Samuel Memorandum was a reasonable basis for a settlement. Here was the same dilemma which had destroyed the Triple Alliance on 'Black Friday', 1921, when the railwaymen and transport workers refused to support the miners after disagreements about who should sit at the negotiating table. Unresolved still, it once again spelt disaster for the miners.

A TUC deputation went to Downing Street early on the afternoon of 12 May. They were not received by the Prime Minister until he had been assured that they came to call off the strike. 'Thank God for your decision', exclaimed Baldwin. 'I shall do all I can to ensure a just and lasting settlement.' Bevin pressed Baldwin for concrete assurances about victimization and ending the lock-out, but without avail. When the conclusion was announced confusion spread among the strikers, many of whom briefly revived the strike unofficially. Accusations of betrayal,

Mrs Churchill congratu-lates Stanley Baldwin on the collapse of the strike

The end of the General Strike. (*Left*) Ernest Bevin, one of the leading TUC negotiators, leaves 10 Downing Street. (*Right*) Henderson, MacDonald and Ben Tillet set off to meet Baldwin to arrange a settlement

inevitable where there was no agreed objective or chain of command, embittered the union scene.

The miners fought on hopeless and alone for six months after the collapse of the General Strike. The owners, knowing time was on their side, had only to sit tight and wait for victory. In November exhaustion and often near-starvation brought final capitulation and District Associations were left to settle as best they could. It was a terrible end of the miners' battle. In the bleak years ahead earnings were to fall even lower and unemployment rose to tragic proportions.

Not all Labour leaders shared the same memory and picture of the General Strike, but nearly all agreed in their hearts – never again! The strike had to some extent been, as Beatrice Webb described it, 'a proletarian distemper which had to run its course'. That course was run – at a cost of £4 million in union funds and diminished union membership and morale.

From 1926 onward the British trade union movement obeyed its more cautious instincts, and made sure it never again found itself in a position where it had no alternative to industrial action on a national scale. The unions had learned that a general strike could not succeed without revolution and there was no prospect of a successful revolution in 1926 or afterwards. They could not afford to follow the mere slogan-izers of 'direct action' and they looked once more to the Labour Party as the constitutional vehicle of progress.

The Conservatives behaved with characteristic maladroitness after the strike. In particular the 1927 Trade Disputes Act was positively vindictive towards the Labour Movement. It made large-scale sympathetic strikes illegal, curtailed peaceful picketing, compelled civil service unions to disaffiliate from the T U C, and replaced 'contracting out' from the political levy by 'contracting in'. The last provision was intended to ruin the Labour Party financially. In the short run it nearly succeeded. Affiliated membership from the unions fell by 1,300,000 to two million and income from affiliation fees was reduced by over a quarter. But like Taff Vale and the Osborne Judgment, it had a boomerang effect, provoking the Party and the unions to work with renewed zeal for a Labour Government.

Chapter Seven

THE SECOND LABOUR GOVERNMENT

Labour's opportunity for revenge came in the late spring of 1929. Baldwin dissolved Parliament at the beginning of May, after a soft budget, and once the new electoral register had come into force containing the 'flappers' – young women voters enfranchised by the 1928 Representation Act; in a total electorate of twenty-nine million, women now outnumbered men by one and a half million. Labour had grounds for optimism, having made a net gain of ten seats in by-elections since 1924. The Party also stood to benefit from the issues of peace and unemployment (never below nine per cent since 1924) which dominated a dull election campaign. The Conservatives placarded the country with portraits of the Prime Minister over the slogans 'Trust Baldwin' and 'Safety First'. Most people did trust Baldwin but many were also a little bored by a leader who, in the words of one senior civil servant, 'believed that happiness for a country consisted in having no history'.

On the day of the count it was soon clear that Britain had turned towards Labour. MacDonald travelled back from the north in triumph. Hugh Dalton, who had just been elected for Bishop Auckland and was to be Under-Secretary at the Foreign Office in the new Administration, was on the same train and recorded that 'at each stop, York, Doncaster, Grantham, great crowds gather on the platforms, cheering and calling for a speech, and we buy new editions of the evening papers and our

LABOUR'S APPEAL TO THE NATION
(See Page Seven)

Daily Herald

SPECIAL GENERAL ELECTION EDITION

THE FIRST LABOUR GOVERNMENT
By J. R. CLYNES, M.P.
(See Page Six)

SPECIAL GENERAL ELECTION EDITION. LONDON, MAY, 1929. ONE PENNY.

WHY LABOUR IS WINNING THE ELECTION.

SHADOW OF FAILURE OVER TORIES

All-Conquering Ideals of the People's Party

FIGHT FOR PEACE

"Our Women Will Not Give Their Children to the Sword"

IN this thrilling call to action Mr. Ramsay MacDonald, Labour's first Prime Minister, writes with withering scorn of the failures of the Tories at home and abroad. "We have a great cause to champion," he declares, "and to cheer after victory."

Labour, he says, seeks to build up from the chaos of Capitalism a community united in life, co-operative in service, mutual in helpfulness.

On the all-important question of preventing future wars, the Leader of the Labour Party indicates that he and his colleagues will strive day-in day-out to aid those women who have vowed that they will not give their children to the sword.

"We can make this election," he declares, "the beginning of a new volume in the history of our country."

By RAMSAY MACDONALD

The great fight has begun.

I appeal for a spirited attack all along the line. He wins who believes he will. The buoyant heart conquers.

Our opponents are dispirited. They have confidence neither in their cause, nor in themselves, nor in their leaders. There is no "Angel of Mons" for them.

The shadow of great failure is over them—failure with the unemployed, failure with the distressed areas, failure at Geneva, failure at home and abroad.

The weapons to which they trusted, like the De-rating Bill, have shrivelled up in their hands. The millions they have added to the register have no gratitude for them because they know that the Government only yielded to the pressure created by others.

WIDOWS CHEATED

The widows to whom pensions have been given have nothing to thank them for, but will vote to include in the pension lists thousands in like distress to themselves who have been turned away empty owing to the senseless conditions imposed by the Tories in the teeth of our pleas for justice.

Lovers of peace are appalled by the obstacles which the Government has put in the way of arbitration and disarmament and by its blindness to the dangers of the present situation.

LABOUR'S GREAT CAUSE

Till the last ballot-box is closed we must fight. We must take nothing for granted. Over-confidence and indifference alike prevent victory.

We face rich parties, parties with a great Press, parties with the tyrannical power of punishment and boycott. Let us meet each with spirit.

There must be no inferiority complex weakening our strokes. Let them slander; let them misrepresent; let them bring out their flaming-eyed and knock-kneed bogies. Let them blare with their trombones and start their stunts. We have a great cause to champion and to cheer after victory.

And what is that cause?

Its programme has been published from the house-tops, and I need not go over its items here once more. We care for something deeper than programmes, however.

Dictatorships are anathema to us. We value most what is behind them, the ideas and ideals which form them. The Labour Party is in truth the people's party. It concerns itself with human life and experience.

It challenges a state of society in which economic power rules men and the conveniences and interests of profiteering determine whether men live in comfort and freedom or in hardship and servitude.

It seeks to build up from the chaos of capitalism a community united in life, co-operative in service, mutual in helpfulness—a community in which the grace of beauty as well as the economic means of life will be within the reach of all who play their part in maintaining and enriching their state.

A WARLESS WORLD

That is our Socialism, and if people say that that is only a dream, and has nothing to do with politics, what is that but what blind and rash dogmatists who swore that there could be nothing new under the sun would have said half a century ago about motor-cars, flying machines, wireless?

With that we link up peace. Our Socialism cannot live in an armed world encamped permanently on the edge of the battlefield.

Our women will not continue to give their children to the sword. We work for a world from which the dread of war has passed, and the assurance that right will be done by reason has taken its place.

We shall substitute the judge for the general. We shall strive to create amongst the nations the habits and responsibilities of neighbourliness, and in every international council and conference we shall champion that policy.

"NO REVOLUTION"

We shall do this by political action. We know of no revolution except that of public opinion using the ballot boxes to elect governments with power to carry out the popular will. We believe in democracy.

Our allies are the Trade Union and the Co-operative Movements, and our friends are those who have a human and moral conception of society.

Such are the underlying issues of the fight in which we join. We can make it the beginning of a new volume of the history of our country. In the years to come it can well be that men will date events from it.

The election of 1929 can be made like to the founding of Rome. This is no extravagance of the imagination but sober fact. It depends upon us. We enter it with every encouragement.

Let us end it with victory!

WOMEN REPRESENTATIVES OF LABOUR

Miss Susan Lawrence — Miss Bondfield — Miss Lee — Miss Wilkinson — Mrs. Dalton

WOMEN AND POLITICS

Wrongs That Injure Home and Child

THE REMEDY

Why Mothers Must Vote Labour

Miss Susan Lawrence (seen above with the four other Labour women M.P.s in the 1924-29 Parliament) makes below a moving appeal to women to vote Labour for the sake of the children.

By SUSAN LAWRENCE

What are the wrongs which press hardest upon women?

The special duty of the normal, happily married woman is in the home; and the very centre of her life is in the bringing up of children. What chance has she got now to fulfil that duty?

First, what sort of a home can she get? The hoardings tell us that there are plenty of houses. This must be meant for the drawing-rooms. There are plenty of houses—just as there are plenty of diamond necklaces; but most of them might as well be in the moon for all the good they are to the workers. Those that can buy houses by instalments are getting housed at the expense of tremendous sacrifices; those who cannot are getting, in many places, worse crowded together every day.

A QUESTION OF MONEY

And the want of good intention is apparent here. Houses can be built for money; it is wholly and solely a question of money. And this Government cut down the housing subsidy. It checked the supply of houses, which was already slow enough. Twice as many houses for letting were built the year before the subsidy was taken off as the year after.

But let us leave the houses, and turn to health. Mr. Chamberlain has told us plainly that he cut down the milk grant for nursing and expectant mothers, "in view of the general need for economy."

The Government had relieved the super-taxed; it had to save the money somewhere. So it took a drop of milk from the babies.

And there are other things which affect mothers and babies. There are new provisions with regard to all public *hospitals*. Formerly local authorities, Poor Law guardians, and town councils could charge what they liked. Some gave treatment free; others made a fixed charge. Now, they must recover as much of the whole cost of treatment as the father, grandfather, mother, grandmother, husband, or children can reasonably pay! They must go—that is, all round the family—and inquire into all their wages, and assess them.

TOO FEW SCHOOLS

But let us turn to another subject. Health is not all; the mother thinks of the character and the moral health of her growing children.

What about the growing boys and girls who leave school and cannot get employment? It is hard enough for a grown man to keep his courage and self-respect during long unemployment. The young are not strong enough for such a trial. There are thousands of boys without work or school or even opportunity for healthy amusement. The schools under the Ministry of Labour are far too few.

We could say much more; these are but a few of the things that women, if they wish, can alter. We ask you to think of these things, and to resolve that for the sake of the home, and the children, and the next generation, you will resolve to end the evil tyranny which presses on the helpless, and give us a Labour Government to make our country happy and prosperous.

SUPERB OPPORTUNITY FOR THE WORKERS

Trades Union Congress Asks For Service to Labour Cause

The following statement is specially contributed by Mr. Ben Tillett and Mr. Walter Citrine, chairman and secretary respectively of the Trades Union Congress.

May of this year has a special significance for trade unionists. It comes on the eve of a General Election which promises to the cause of Labour *a great victory for a great faith*. Let it be for all working men and women a month of resolution. Let them firmly resolve that they will leave no stone unturned, no effort unaccomplished which may result in the triumph of Labour's case.

They have the opportunity and the power to make an end of the most reactionary and indolent Government of modern times.

It has sought to cripple Trade Unionism by the infamous Act of 1927. It has handicapped the unemployed by an increasing rigour on the administration of benefits. It has lengthened the working day for over a million miners.

It has done little to increase the supply of houses which working-class families can rent, little for maternity and child welfare, little for education. Its foreign policy has been an abysmal failure.

Its one thought in taxation has been to lighten the burden upon the rich. It has now the temerity to ask from the country a renewal of confidence for a policy of stagnation.

The Trades Union Congress General Council calls upon toilers everywhere to work with vigorous determination for the return of a Labour Government to power. It asks from them a people's government for a people's cause.

A Labour Government in power

MR. BEN TILLETT

means peace abroad and progress at home.

It means disarmament and security built upon international goodwill.

It means promoting economic revival by international confidence.

Every vote for Labour is a vote for peace.

The Trades Union Congress General Council reminds its members that a Labour victory holds for them the promise of a policy fitted to their needs and made by men and women who know those needs, because they themselves have endured them.

A vote for Labour means the emancipation of the trade unions. A vote for Labour means the reorganisation of the mining industry.

A vote for Labour means the tackling of unemployment in a spirit of constructive determination.

It means not empty promises but definite and helpful performance. It means self-government by a people determined to be free.

The occasion is momentous; the opportunity is superb. Let us grasp

MR. CITRINE

with courage and determination the chance to be masters of the event.

Every vote for Labour is a vote for the workers' freedom.

VIEWS OF A FREE CHURCHMAN

"I Believe in Labour's Policy"

"I shall vote Labour," writes the Rev. A. D. Belden, of Whitefield's, Tottenham Court-road, London, "at this election because Labour is the only party that proposes to restore the natural human (and divine) right of the public in the Resources of Nature—the objective source of wealth.

Rev. A. D. Belden

"It is the only party that proposes to put economic resource adequately behind every citizen, thus liberating enterprise and energy—the subjective source of wealth.

"Only such a policy, wisely and progressively pursued, will remove the toll of luxury, idleness, and waste now levied upon the nation's resources, and provide both work and wealth for all at last.

"I believe Socialism to be the economic expression of Christianity. It will provide institutions of society in contrast to those now existing which will give hope and encouragement to the positive Christian virtues, instead of appealing to the lower incentives.

"I believe the Labour Party to be more thorough in its devotion to International Peace and the Abolition of War than any other Party."

'Flappers', women over twenty-one and under thirty, have their first opportunity to vote, 1929

The women of Stepney going to the polls

gains go mounting up. . . . At King's Cross at 11.00 p.m. a vast crowd, cheering like mad outside the station. We go home to bed.' They awoke next day to find Labour had 288 seats and was for the first time the largest party in Parliament. Also for the first time non-trade union members were a majority of the Parliamentary Party. But it would still be in a minority of the House if the fifty-nine Liberals voted with the 260 Tories. Once more MacDonald and his colleagues had to shoulder the burdens of office without the majority to give them real power.

◀ (Left) The front page of the 1929 election edition of the Daily Herald

The composition of the Government was decided after discussions among the 'Big Five' – MacDonald, Henderson, Snowden, Thomas and Clynes. A dozen of the new Cabinet had served there in 1924, six of them in the same posts, so there was adequate continuity of experience. Among the newcomers were Arthur Greenwood as Minister of Health, Wedgwood Benn as Secretary for India, and Margaret Bondfield, the first woman member of the Cabinet, and not a complete success, at the Ministry of Labour. Most significant was the disappointment of the left wing. Wheatley and F. W. Jowett, both from the I L P and Cabinet Ministers in 1924, were not included this time – omissions not fully compensated by the inclusion of George Lansbury in minor office. Mac-Donald was seeking the middle ground of politics. The programme laid down in the Address from the throne at the opening of the new Parliament was strikingly cautious. Speaking in support of it, Mac-Donald asked the House: 'I wonder how far it is possible, without in any way abandoning any of our party positions . . . to consider ourselves more as a Council of State and less as arrayed regiments facing each other in battle . . . so far as we are concerned, co-operation will be welcomed.'

Labour's successful
Minister of Transport,
Herbert Morrison,
opening a bridge

Not very much co-operation was forthcoming in the two years ahead. The Bill to amend the hated 1927 Trades Unions Act was so mutilated in committee that it had to be withdrawn. Charles Trevelyan's Education Bill foundered on the question of Church schools. A Coal Mines Act was passed, cartellizing the industry, but it was greatly amended in committee and in the Lords, where clauses to raise a levy to aid weaker mines and to enforce amalgamation of colliery companies were rejected. Measures for land utilization, for reform of the electoral system, to set up a Consumers Council, and to ratify the Washington Forty-eight Hours Convention were held up until lost at the fall of the Government. Yet despite these failures the early work of Labour's second Government promised well enough. In the social welfare field the pensions of widows and aged were improved and extended, unemployment insurance was made more easily available and slum clearance quickened. Herbert Morrison soon made his mark with a bill to reorganize road passenger transport. William Graham at the Board of

The Labour Cabinet, 1929. *Seated:* J.R. Clynes, Lord Parmoor, J.H. Thomas, P. Snowden, Ramsay MacDonald, Arthur Henderson, Sidney Webb, Lord Justice Sankey, Wedgewood Benn. *Standing:* George Lansbury, A.V. Alexander, C.P. Trevelyan, M. Bondfield, Lord Thomson, Tom Shaw, A. Greenwood, Noel Buxton, W. Graham, W. Adamson

Trade moved the world's trading nations closer towards a tariff truce. The Indian Statutory Commission, on which Atlee served prominently, reported progress in 1930 – though not enough to satisfy the hopes of many. Above all, Henderson emerged as a Foreign Secretary of great stature, striving for international co-operation and disarmament; in these efforts he received active and able support from MacDonald.

But one problem remained intractable. Labour had emphasized all along that ending unemployment was the most important task before it. It now found itself incapable of carrying this out. J.H. Thomas, Lansbury and Oswald Mosley, the Ministers concerned, proved an unhappy team. Public works schemes totalling some £135 million

Failures... and successes

107

An unemployment demonstration during the 1930 Depression

Unemployment were authorized, but would make little impression for some time ahead – and there proved to be no time to wait, for events beyond the Government's control were rushing the country into crisis. Britain's economic outlook had never been particularly bright during the later 1920s. Its share of world trade had fallen considerably since 1924 and prices and profit margins continued to shrink, discouraging investment. In the summer of 1929 the long American industrial boom, which Europe had envied and Americans thought permanent, ended and shortly after came the catastrophic Wall Street crash. The collapse of its most powerful unit exposed the weaknesses in the world economy – especially the surplus supply of primary products and the excessive dependence of some European countries on American credit. Britain was inevitably involved in the chain reaction. Prices and levels of world trade fell, and with them the value and profitability of Britain's exports. New capital investment declined abruptly. Unemployment – 9·6 per cent when Labour took office – had risen to almost 20 per cent by the end of 1930. Mosley and Lansbury put up a programme, based on expanding demand in the home market and insulating Britain from foreign competition, which promised to alleviate the crisis at home. But

Mosley's programme

108

Snowden led the Cabinet in rejecting it; whereupon Mosley resigned from the Government (and Attlee succeeded him as Chancellor of the Duchy of Lancaster).

Oswald Mosley

Disquiet about the mounting unemployment was reflected at the 1930 Llandudno Conference. Maxton moved an ILP amendment denouncing the Government for its 'timidity and vacillation in refusing to apply socialist remedies' – naming wholesale nationalization as an essential solution. This was rejected after heated exchanges between Maxton and Wise on one side and MacDonald and Clynes on the other. But many trade union moderates also expressed concern at the gloom and despair facing the one in five of their members who were without a job and the Conference carried a motion put by the General Workers calling for much more positive action. Mosley himself spoke at the Conference. He was well received and was elected to the National Executive as a local parties representative. He continued afterwards to agitate within the Labour Party, building himself up as a leader of the left wing, closely supported by John Strachey and Aneurin Bevan. But before long his over-reaching ambitions led him to break from Labour to form the New Party. He later became the führer of British fascism and began to fight those on the left he had so recently sought to lead.

Oswald Mosley, founder of the New Party and soon to turn to fascism, addressing an election meeting

Lansbury's lido at Hyde Park. (*Top right*) choosing a site; (*left*) by the bathing huts; (*bottom right*) opening day

J.M. Keynes

The original unemployment team did not long survive Mosley's departure. Thomas was moved to the quieter waters of the Dominions Office. Lansbury devoted himself entirely to extending public ameni-ties – his lido in Hyde Park being a popular memorial to his work. MacDonald now took over personal supervision of unemployment; but the situation continued to worsen. During 1931 the percentage of those out of work remained above twenty per cent. MacDonald brought the Liberals into informal policy discussions, though this only added to the existing administrative confusion, with a complex of committees and no clear co-ordinating direction. A high-powered Economic Advisory Council was in existence, including J. M. Keynes, the great Liberal economist, and representatives of employers and unions, but it met only rarely – less often as the situation grew worse and never after the spring of 1931.

As the Government drifted, the one Labour leader clear and firm in his path was the Chancellor of the Exchequer, Snowden. Unfortun-

Snowden leaves Downing Street to present his first Budget, 1930

ately his policies were not well-suited to mitigate the economic storm which was striking Britain. Snowden remained obstinately committed to free trade and the gold standard. He sought with Gladstonian perseverance to balance the budget and keep up the Sinking Fund for the repayment of the National Debt. Financial orthodoxy became for him a question of moral rectitude. But maintaining the gold standard meant that any fall in world prices inevitably forced down British export prices – and hence wage levels. The maintenance of free trade allowed other countries to try to solve their own economic problems by dumping cut-price goods on the already sluggish British market. The attempt to balance the budget and the refusal to suspend Sinking Fund payments meant that social expenditure had to be cut. The price of financial orthodoxy was to be paid by lowering the living standards of the British working people. It was being exacted by a Labour Government nurtured and brought to power over thirty years with the main purpose of protecting those people.

Snowden's financial orthodoxy

Nobody in the Cabinet had the financial expertise, or possibly the necessary courage, to oppose Snowden in his policy of retrenchment. He did not lack outside encouragement, from Whitehall, the City, the press and the political Opposition. The most important support came from the 'May Committee' report on Public Expenditure in June 1931. Snowden chose to ignore completely the fact that its two Labour representatives had refused to sign it and had submitted a minority report. He fully accepted the gloomy forecasts of a huge budget deficit and impending economic disaster made by its five businessmen representatives. They recommended immediate cuts in unemployment benefit, in public works schemes, and in teachers', police and service pay totalling almost £100 million.

Snowden's primary purpose in setting up this committee was to prepare British opinion for the severe economic retrenchment to which he was already committed. The immediate effect was to convince foreign holders of sterling that Britain was on the brink of bankruptcy.

These foreign depositors were already enmeshed in the international financial crisis which had been gaining momentum since the American crash of 1929 and the consequent suspension of transatlantic credit to Europe. First the Austrian and then the German banks had to freeze their assets and appeal for international assistance. Confidence in European finance fell and liquidity was reduced. Other countries

During 1931 there were many demonstrations by public servants such as these post office workers to protest against cuts in their pay

turned to London for funds and France repatriated her balances. London began to lose gold at an alarming rate – nearly £2½ million a day during the last two weeks of July 1931. Large loans were negotiated in New York and Paris by the Bank of England – but only on condition that social expenditure was cut along the lines of the May Report. Step by step the Cabinet agreed to a succession of economies to placate the bankers. Given the crisis, given the maintenance of the gold standard and free trade, then the loans had to be raised and the conditions met. But in the end, on 23 August 1931, a rump of nine or ten in the *Cabinet split* Cabinet, encouraged from the outside by the TUC, dug in their heels against slashing unemployment benefits. They were unable to put up adequate arguments against Snowden on this, as on any other complex economic issue. But they felt, economic logic or not, that a Labour Government must not execute a policy so hostile to its own people.

MacDonald could not continue against the resistance of nearly half *MacDonald* his Cabinet. He asked for everyone's resignation and went for an *resigns* audience with the King, who summoned a conference for the next day with MacDonald and the other two party leaders, Baldwin and Samuel. After that Conference the Labour ex-ministers gathered, expecting to learn that the Conservative Opposition was to take over. But MacDonald announced that a National Government was to be formed with himself as Prime Minister and Baldwin and Samuel

MacDonald's coalition, as seen by *Punch*

"WI' MACDONALD, SIR DONALD, SAM (HERBERT), SAM HOARE, JIM THOMAS, STAN' BALDWIN, OLD UNCLE PHIL SNOWDEN AND ALL."

A Cabinet meeting of the National Government

serving under him. Apparently he offered little or no explanation. The stunned gathering soon broke up – except for Snowden, Thomas and Lord Sankey who were kept behind to be offered posts in the new Administration. The second Labour Government was at an end. The first 'had been destroyed by a Red Letter', Dalton told a meeting of the Parliamentary Party on 28 August 1931, 'the second by a Banker's Order'. But this was an over-simplification which ignored Labour's responsibility for its own failures.

Confusion and deep conflicts of personal loyalty were produced by MacDonald's action. But the traditional solidity of the trade unions helped to stabilize the movement. The unions had been much clearer than the Cabinet in opposing Snowden's policies. A TUC delegation to Downing Street on 20 August had told MacDonald and Snowden that further deflation was no solution to a recession – a view which later economic experience seems to confirm, but was then confined to Bevin, Keynes, Mosley and a few maverick economists. Bevin had a leading hand in this approach, as he had in convening a meeting with Citrine, Lansbury, Henderson and Jim Middleton, assistant Secretary of the Party, the day after the National Government was formed. They decided to go into opposition and managed to swing the *Daily Herald* over to their point of view. This opposition was confirmed by an official resolution passed by a joint meeting of the Parliamentary Party and the General Council of the TUC on 26 August. Two days later Henderson was elected leader and on 28 September 1931 MacDonald and those Labour MPs who followed him were formally expelled from the Party by the National Executive.

The Labour Movement never forgave MacDonald for his alleged desertion and later tended to put upon him all the blame for the disastrous failure of the 1929–31 Government. In fact the whole Cabinet

Labour betrayed?

Arthur Henderson, elected as leader
to succeed MacDonald

had shared in the drift into crisis and then approved the retrenchment decisions right until the last straw of cutting unemployment insurance. It must also be said for MacDonald that he may well have been completely sincere in his belief that he was acting for the public good in agreeing to form a National Government. But this does not mean that he was right. For he made little attempt to explain his actions and then persisted in carrying out a policy repudiated by the party he was elected to lead. He showed little sense of loyalty to the Labour Movement and in the subsequent election campaign joined Snowden in contemptuous denigration of their former colleagues. Personal vanity and the 'aristocratic embrace' of the society circles in which he lately moved, are often put forward as the explanation of MacDonald's 'treachery'. Snowden, though he never shared MacDonald's liking for Tory high living, was also said by Beatrice Webb to have undergone a change of character: 'from being a fervent apostle of Utopian Socialism, thirty years of parliamentary life and ten years of Front Bench politics have made him the upholder of the banker, the landed aristocrat and the Crown'. But perhaps we shall never know with confidence what motives moved these two men, or indeed influenced some of their opponents, during the final crisis days in August 1931. For many questions remained in doubt and dispute.

Was there really a terrible financial crisis, or just a convenient emergency – a 'banker's ramp' to destroy the Labour Government? Had MacDonald been long preparing to change horses in mid-stream? Did he at first sincerely believe that the National Government would last only until the economic position was restored and that there would be no election under the Coalition? What was the constitutional role of George V in initiating the National Government? Were the other Labour ministers as solidly and immediately opposed to MacDonald's action as they later went to great pains to suggest? Whatever the answers, this was a sad, even tragic end for MacDonald. He was to enjoy the trappings of highest office for nearly four more years. But a lifetime's dedicated work for Labour was dashed from the movement's collective memory by a storm of hatred at his action in August 1931.

The Labour Party went away to a sad annual Conference at

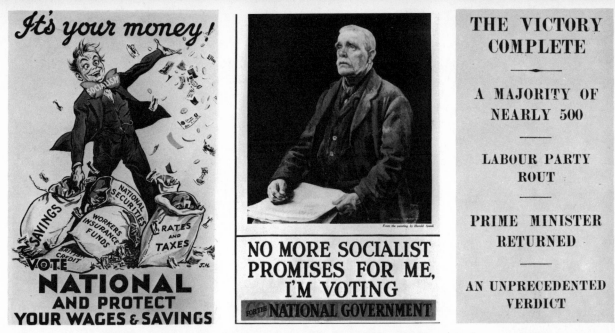

National Government posters hasten the rout of Labour *(right, The Times)* in the 1931 election

Scarborough in early October. Before it was closed the National Government announced the dissolution of Parliament. The election campaign was bitter; it was described by the *Manchester Guardian* as 'the most fraudulent campaign of modern times'.

For the first time ever Labour's poll fell compared with the previous election – by nearly two million votes. Moreover, because of coalitions of Liberals and Conservatives against it, the number of Labour MPs fell disproportionately – from 289 to 46. The Party was almost back to the level of 1910. Its leadership was decimated. Only three ex-ministers were returned – Lansbury, Attlee and Cripps. MacDonald had gone to the country asking for 'a doctor's mandate' and he was given a majority of 500 over all other parties. 471 of his following were Conservatives returned under the Coalition label. One of the few consolations for Labour was that no substantial bloc of the Party took up their late leader's banner. Sir William Jowitt, Clifford Allen and a few other Labour Members and Peers followed MacDonald, Snowden and Thomas. But at the election 'National Labour' had no popular support; its few successes were because of coalition support. The Labour Party was bloody but still basically united.

Transport House, built as the headquarters of the Transport and General Workers Union in 1928. Part of it became the Labour Party Headquarters later in the same year

Chapter Eight

THE WILDERNESS

The years after 1931 were dominated by economic depression at home and the increasing military aggression of the dictators abroad. These two issues, threatening work and peace, touched the heart of Labour's deepest aspirations. Yet Labour could do little to influence the course of events. The 1931 crisis had not substantially divided the movement, as was at first feared, but for a time it knocked the stuffing out of the Parliamentary Party. Its leading figures were gone, either defeated at the polls or lost to the National Government. That Government, 'national' in name but Conservative in men and measures, had for the next nine years an overwhelming majority which would have empowered it to do anything, but in the event simply permitted it to do little.

The Labour Opposition in the Commons fumed impotently at MacDonald, at Baldwin and at Neville Chamberlain in turn. Its own leadership situation was far from satisfactory. Henderson, who was out of the Commons, resigned in 1932 and was succeeded by Lansbury. But Lansbury was, at seventy-two, too old to lead a political counter-attack, and as a complete religious pacifist, he was unable to subscribe to some of the policies of the party he was supposed to lead. His chief lieutenants, Attlee and Sir Stafford Cripps, a rich and left-wing lawyer, had not yet established themselves properly in the movement. Behind them was a demoralized and unrepresentative following, a third from

South Wales and a half from the miners' union. Because of these weaknesses, in the first half of the 1930s Parliament was something of a backwater in Labour affairs. The main focus of activity was the annual Conference, where the whole movement gathered, including the trade unions, who had resumed, since the last days of the 1931 crisis, a leading political role. In particular Bevin, the Bristol drayman who was building up the Transport and General Workers Union to a dominant place in the trade union movement, often dominated Labour's political stage.

Trade union leadership

Perhaps inevitably there was after 1931 some pressure to push the Party to the left. Many wished to dissociate themselves from MacDonald and the kind of compromises with the right which he was felt to represent. The ILP in 1932 pressed this dissociation to the point of disaffiliation: a sad parting of a founder member after a sometimes stormy though always fruitful partnership. The immediate point at issue between them concerned the reluctance of ILP members to accept the discipline of Labour Party standing orders in the Commons. But the gulf between the two had long been wide and ever-widening. Throughout the 1920s the ILP had been convinced that Labour's moderation, constitutionalism and pragmatism was wrong. It saw 'MacDonaldism' as the natural evolution from that policy and the catastrophe of 1931 as the inevitable result. The ILP now followed its more extreme inclinations and issued a new 'Statement of Policy' which announced the (ever) imminent downfall of capitalism and called for renewed class militancy and 'mass industrial action' in the coming struggle to 'replace capitalism by the Socialist Commonwealth'. But the British workers did not share this apocalyptic vision. Disaffiliation meant suicide for the ILP, not the millennium for Britain. Its membership fell from 17,000 to little over 4,000 in the next three years. However, the advocates of militant socialism within the Party soon found a new rally in the Socialist League, in which Cripps, Frank Wise, Brailsford and Harold Laski, the LSE political scientist, played prominent roles.

The ILP secession

The early 1930s were not completely barren for Labour. Particularly encouraging in 1934 was the capture of the LCC, which made Herbert Morrison's reputation as a constructive reformer and was to remain

Stafford Cripps, Ernest Bevin and Clement Attlee, three rising leaders of the Labour Party, in the early 1930s. Attlee (*below*) speaks on unemployment in Hyde Park. Will Thorne is on his left

New policies

a shining example of Labour administration for the next thirty years. At Transport House the Party had quickly set about rebuilding its policies for the future. The fruits of its rethinking were seen in a series of policy documents, culminating in 1937 with *Labour's Immediate Programme*, which sold three-quarters of a million copies, then a record sale for a party pamphlet. They were supplemented by the valuable research done by the New Fabian Research Bureau, which was active throughout the 1930s and finally merged with and rejuvenated the then moribund Fabian Society. Next time Labour entered office it would know in some detail what it intended to do and how it proposed to do it.

In domestic affairs Labour's greatest concern was with unemployment. The economy had deteriorated further in the first twelve months of the National Government, but the worst of the depression was over by 1933. Between then and 1937, as world trade picked up again, the volume of production rose nearly fifty per cent and real wages rose

The hunger marches: Ellen Wilkinson leading the Jarrow unemployed through Hyde Park after their long march to London

James Maxton opens the national headquarters of the disaffiliated and declining
Independent Labour Party in 1934

sharply. Unemployment fell from a peak of three million (twenty-three   *On the dole*
per cent of insured persons) at the beginning of 1933 to a plateau of
one and three-quarter million between 1937 and 1939. But this plateau
concealed a terrible concentration of unemployment in some areas
dependent upon depressed industries like coal and shipbuilding. In
1935 over sixty per cent of the insured workers of Merthyr Tydfil and
over seventy per cent of those in Jarrow were unemployed. The march
to London of Jarrow unemployed led by Ellen Wilkinson was only one
of the many demonstrations and hunger marches in various parts of
Britain. The tragedy lay not only in the numbers but also in the length
of time they had been unemployed. In 1936 nearly three-quarters of the
unemployed in Crook in County Durham and half of those in the
Rhondda had been out of work for over five years. The older men came
to believe that they would never earn another week's pay – and the
young ones that they would never earn their first. They were humiliated

by enforced idleness and by the petty administration of the dole with its means test, by which they eked out a miserable existence.

The effect on all who experienced or saw this unemployment was to make them swear it must never happen again. It conditioned the voting of many normally non-Labour voters in 1945 and the thinking and actions of the Labour Government after then. But Labour could do very little while impotent in Parliamentary opposition. This situation of hopelessness and despair was exploited equally and similarly by the *Fascism* fascist Right and the communist Left. Each denounced democracy as a sham, derided the Labour Party as a failure, and sought a solution through revolution. The fascists obtained great publicity by their violence, their anti-semitism, and their theatrical leader, Mosley. But their followers probably never exceeded 25,000. Communist membership was even lower, though the Party's appeal and objectives were more stable than the fascists, who were in time discredited by the actions of Hitler and Mussolini abroad. On the whole, considering the conditions

Fascist violence in London's East End, 1936

The Labour Party, the TUC and the Co-operative Union jointly decided on a boycott of German goods in protest against Nazism

under which they suffered, the British working people remained remarkably resistant to appeals to extremism from whatever direction.

As the economic situation at home improved, the world political scene darkened. Hitler became Chancellor of Germany in 1933 and soon destroyed the trade unions and withdrew his country from the League of Nations. In 1934 the Austrian socialists were overthrown and the Geneva Disarmament Conference died, despite Henderson's passionate struggle to make it succeed. In the following year Hitler introduced conscription in Germany, a prelude to his occupation of the Rhineland, and Mussolini prepared to launch a murderous attack on Abyssinia. This brutal advance of fascism presented Labour with a dilemma. For though most people in the movement wished to see fascism stopped, many were not at first willing to face up to the implications – that force might have to be met by force. Some held Lansbury's complete Christian pacifist position: nothing justified the use of force and nothing but evil could come of its use. Some supported Cripps in the Marxist view that the workers must not participate in any war but the

Labour's pacifism

125

class war. Many had much vaguer pacifist views which were more difficult to combat because they were less open and definite than those of Cripps or Lansbury. They wanted resistance but would not contemplate force, they approved sanctions but not armaments, the ultimate instruments of sanctions. They knew Hitler had to be stopped, but felt a profound distaste for the means necessary to stop him, especially when put at the disposal of a reactionary Conservative Government. They hoped that by denouncing fascism it would somehow go away, and by passionately and sincerely longing for peace the war would be avoided. Part of their emotional attachment to the League until the bitter end was that it gave hope of security without reverting to armed action. These people were the harder to lead towards harsh reality because they were often attached to the Labour Movement through a common desire for a peaceful world. The horrors of 1914–18 and the cynicism of the post-war settlement were embedded in their memories. Those too young to remember had their imaginations sharpened by the spate of anti-war books brought out in the 1930s by such writers as Robert Graves, Siegfried Sassoon, Beverley Nichols, Vera Brittain and Richard Aldington. 'They had preached the iniquity of war and armaments so long,' as Josiah Wedgwood wrote of his colleagues in the Commons, that faced by the new threat of Nazism, 'many wilfully shut their eyes and brains'.

Mussolini's invasion of Abyssinia in the autumn of 1935 occasioned a sharp Party dispute at a singularly unfortunate time. The TUC, following the clear and decisive lead of Bevin and Citrine, had voted in favour of resisting Mussolini by whatever means necessary, risking war if need be, and the National Executive had prepared a resolution for the Brighton Conference along these lines. But serious difficulties arose. Lansbury, leader of the Parliamentary Party, publicly campaigned against the strong policy line, Ponsonby resigned from the leadership of the Party in the Lords, and Cripps from the National Executive. Lansbury, speaking of his faith that 'God intended us to live peaceably and quietly with one another', opposed the Executive at Brighton and the Conference gave him a marvellous and affectionate reception. Then Ernest Bevin strode to the rostrum and cut, brutally at times, through

(*Left*) The pacifist George Lansbury. (*Right*) Clement Attlee speaks at an anti-Nazi meeting

the emotional foliage of Lansbury's appeal and through the intellectual sophistries of Cripps. Many at the Conference bitterly resented his style of attack. But they knew he was right and voted massively for the Executive resolution. Lansbury then resigned the leadership. His deputy, Clement Attlee, son of a city solicitor, educated at Haileybury and Oxford, took over in the interim, the first Labour leader not of working-class origins. He was confirmed by ballot, after the election, defeating Herbert Morrison and Arthur Greenwood, and remained in control for the next twenty years.

Attlee leader

Baldwin's Government responded shrewdly, if cynically, to the national mood in 1935. The wider public, as well as Labour supporters, clearly wanted Britain to support the League of Nations and to oppose Mussolini. The 'Peace Ballot', covering eleven and a half million people, showed a majority of 10 to 1 in favour of disarmament and continued support for the League; it also gave a large majority for sanctions against any aggressor. In the autumn Baldwin called an election, in which he stole all of Labour's clothes, declaring his Government fully in support of League sanctions against Mussolini. The

Labour Party was damaged by the resignation of its leaders in both Houses of Parliament on the most important issue of the campaign. On polling day Labour trebled its seats to 154 and its vote, at eight and a quarter million, almost recovered to the 1929 peak. Its front-bench team was strengthened by the return of a number of former Ministers, including Morrison, Dalton and Clynes. The Tories fell from 454 to 387. But Baldwin's majority was still around 250, and this Parliament was to remain in being for another ten years, long after the temporary circumstances which determined its party composition – the popularity of Baldwin, the mistaken belief that he would support the League, the lingering mistrust of Labour since 1931 – had passed away. One outcome gratifying to Labour was the failure of MacDonald's National Labour Party, whose numbers sank to eight. Only J. H. Thomas survived of those who deserted in 1931 (and he was to resign the following year after a budget scandal). MacDonald himself was crushingly defeated by Emanuel Shinwell at Seaham. He found a safe by-election seat shortly after, but was dead within two years. Most Labour members declined invitations to his memorial service in Westminster Abbey.

An ageing MacDonald with J. H. Thomas leaving St James's Palace after a royal reception

The election results are declared (*above*) and Emanuel Shinwell (*centre right*) defeats MacDonald at Seaham Harbour in the 1935 election

Labour MPs set off for Spain in January 1938: Shinwell, Bevan, J.J. Lawson, Tom Williams and W. Paling

Spain – the end of Labour Pacifism

MacDonald's great services to the Party in its formative years were forgotten; his betrayal alone was remembered.

1936 was a watershed for Labour's views on defence and foreign policy. The League, lacking any serious assistance from Britain or France, failed to prevent Mussolini from butchering Abyssinia into submission. It was never again a force on which liberals could sincerely pin their hopes. Also the Spanish Civil War opened, with the insurgents under General Franco invading from North Africa with massive German and Italian assistance to overthrow the legitimate Republican Government. The fate of Spain swung many in the Labour Party away from pacifism and they were now willing to contemplate

Attlee speaks in Trafalgar Square against British recognition of Franco's Government

An anti-appeasement tableau in Labour's May Day rally in Hyde Park, 1938

rearmament. The Parliamentary Party ceased in 1937 to oppose the service vote. That year's Conference, led by Bevin and Dalton against the left wing opposition of Bevan and Cripps, gave massive support to a policy statement demanding adequate rearmament and maximum resistance to the dictators. From now on Labour was able to mount more convincing attacks on the appeasement policies of the new Prime Minister, Chamberlain, who went to Munich in 1938, connived at the destruction of Czechoslovakia, that 'far-away country' as he described it, and returned promising 'peace in our time'. During the few days' Commons debate which followed, Attlee denounced this humiliating act whereby the Czechs had been 'betrayed and handed over to a ruthless despotism'. But even aided by the abstention of Churchill, Eden and the other Tory rebels, Labour could make no impression on the massive Conservative majority – supported, as it undoubtedly was, by a general public relieved to find itself not at war.

As fascism marched remorselessly and brutally on, there arose in Britain demands for a broad coalition of opposition groups to overthrow

Combatting appeasemement

131

the Conservative Government. In January 1937, the Communist Party, the Socialist League and the ILP issued a 'Unity Manifesto' calling for a United Front 'against Fascism, reaction and war'. It was supported by the new weekly *Tribune*, founded by Cripps and G.R. Strauss, two of the richest socialists in Britain, and Aneurin Bevan. Their main target seemed to be the Labour leaders as much as Baldwin or Chamberlain. The Labour National Executive reacted quickly, expelling the Socialist League, which soon dissolved, and reminding the movement to beware of 'sham' unities. 'The real United Front', it declared, 'is that of the Socialist, Trade Union and Co-operative movements.' But the pressure for a broad coalition reappeared in a new form in 1938 with the Popular Front containing Liberals and even some dissident Tories as well as the socialist and communist Left. The Front received support from Victor Gollancz's successful Left Book Club and from *Reynolds News*, recently revitalized under new co-operative ownership. Once again the Party Executive was adamant that it would not join in any coalitions. But it did not keep its separate identity without a battle with Cripps, who had swung from his Marxist adherence to rigid proletarian solidarity to demands for an alliance of all classes. He campaigned against the Party's policy and was finally expelled in the spring of 1939. Bevan and Strauss followed him but soon returned to the Party fold – as did Cripps much later, in 1945.

The vote at the 1939 Labour Party Conference which confirmed that Sir Stafford Cripps should be expelled for his 'Popular Front' activities. Each unit on the cards represents 1,000 members

Richard Crossman, who twenty-five years later became a Labour Cabinet member, canvassing with A.D. Lindsay, Master of Balliol College, Oxford, 'United Front' candidate in the Oxford by-election held shortly after the Munich agreement. Lindsay was defeated by Quintin Hogg who fought on a platform defending Munich.

G.R. Strauss, Lady Cripps, Sir Stafford Cripps and Aneurin Bevan at the 1939 Conference

War　　On 1 September 1939 Hitler invaded Poland and the British Government issued a warning that unless German troops were withdrawn war would be declared. The next day a joint meeting of the National Executive and of the Executive of the Parliamentary Party decided to support the Government in resisting Hitler's aggression. But the Party was not prepared to join in a coalition under Chamberlain; its hostility to him and his colleagues, the 'guilty men' of Munich, was still very strong. Labour gave loyal support to the general prosecution of the war. It readily joined in an electoral truce with the other two parties. It abandoned its opposition to mass conscription. But it preferred to remain uncommitted to the existing Administration in case new men and measures were needed. 'Should there be confused councils, inefficiency and wavering,' warned Greenwood in the Commons, 'then other men must be called to take their places.'

A critical look from a working man as Neville Chamberlain walks in the park with his wife in 1940

The War Cabinet in October 1941. *Seated:* Sir John Anderson, W. Churchill, C.R. Attlee, A. Eden. *Standing:* A. Greenwood, E. Bevin, Beaverbrook, Sir Kingsley Wood

By May 1940 it was clear that other men were urgently needed. When Norway fell in humiliating circumstances, the Labour Party censured the Government and some hundred nominal supporters of the Government abstained or voted with Labour. Chamberlain then approached Attlee to join in a coalition, but the National Executive decided to join only under a new leader. The task fell to Winston Churchill. He offered Labour a very fair share of important offices, with Attlee and Greenwood in the small war Cabinet of five. Bevin and Morrison went to the key Ministries of Labour and Supply, and Dalton, Alexander and Sir William Jowitt also became Ministers.

. . . and into Coalition

135

Ernest Bevin

Healing the
1931 wounds
The events of May 1940 did more than create a Coalition Govern-ment which would eventually win the war. They also finally brought Labour out of the wilderness of opposition, signifying the healing of the wounds inflicted on it in 1931. The effects of that disaster had been to make the Party appear unfit to govern and feel something of a political outsider. Subsequently it was tugged hither and thither by revolu-tionaries of the I L P and the Socialist League, tempted by the Christian pacifism of Lansbury and by the messianic Marxism of Cripps. Throughout these storms the trade unions had been both compass and sheet anchor. Citrine, the able and lucid General Secretary of the T U C, and Bevin, with his stamina, his loyalty, his realistic judgment on people and issues, his instinctive sense of what the British working people wanted, formed a stable centre on which a new political leader-ship could find its balance. Attlee, Morrison, Greenwood and Dalton had by now joined with Bevin to form that leadership, confidently fit to share in government again.

Chapter Nine

A DECADE IN POWER

From Labour's entry into the Coalition in May 1940 until peace in Europe in 1945, party politics effectively ceased and the history of the Labour Party is often indistinguishable from the history of Britain. Even so the war was a watershed of great importance to Labour. It had been out of office for nineteen of the twenty-two years since it became an independent national party in 1918; it was now to be in Government for more than a decade after 1940. Its leaders shared in decision-taking, where in the 1930s they had been quite without influence. The ordinary people of Britain who made up the bulk of party membership felt totally committed to the cause of defeating Hitler, where in the 1930s they had been anaesthetized by the negative policies of those who then ruled. Labour experienced a sense of power, of responsibility and of having a stake in Britain's future.

The present also had its brighter side even in the darkest days of war. Unemployment disappeared. Improvements were made in the welfare services, in hospitals, in school meals and milk for children, in pensions for the old, which had been declared impractical in the less exacting days of peace. Rationing gave fair shares for all; highly progressive taxation secured a redistribution of real income to the poorer people. Government machinery was set up for central economic planning of a kind that Labour had long advocated against Tory scepticism. The

(*Left*) Nine ration books. War-time rationing tended to raise the standard of living of the poorer families, and helped to lay the foundations for the post-war Welfare State

(*Right*) Herbert Morrison as Home Secretary inspects London blitz damage

mines and the railways were brought under direct government control. Indeed it could be said that war went a long way towards bringing about the revolution in society of which Labour had always dreamed. By 1945 Britain was already 'tooled-up' for what was to come after; the Labour Government then had to finish the job.

Labour helps win the war

The position of Labour's Parliamentary leadership was greatly strengthened by its participation in the Coalition Government, for it quickly acquired the national prestige accruing to men successfully directing Britain's affairs. Attlee grew enormously in stature as deputy Prime Minister. Morrison skilfully organized civil defence. Bevin mobilized the nation's work force into the armed services or war production. Dalton energetically ran first economic warfare and then the Board of Trade. Consequently the Parliamentary Party resumed the central direction of the movement which it had effectively ceded to the trade unions after 1931; this transfer of power was personified and emphasized by Ernest Bevin's leap from his union's headquarters into the Cabinet.

(*Left*) Hugh Dalton and Anthony Eden with Dr Benes and Jan Masaryk, the leaders of the exile Czecho-slovak Government in London in 1941

(*Right*) Labour's leaders become known as national leaders

Potential opposition from within the Party was to some extent muted by the circumstances of war. Constitutionally there was now no official Opposition in Parliament and the office of Leader of the Opposition lapsed for the duration – though first Lees-Smith and then Pethick-Lawrence, two senior and reliable party stalwarts, acted as unofficial spokesmen for Labour members not in the Government. Some traditional critics were also constrained to silence by a desire not to appear to be weakening national unity at a time of emergency.

There were, however, exceptions to this consensus of support for the war effort. Aneurin Bevan led a series of frontal attacks on the Coalition throughout the war, and he was supported by a small group of left-wing MPs centred on *Tribune*. Outside the Party, the ILP called upon British workers not to co-operate in an imperialist war. The Communists shared this view, attempting to sabotage war production by fomenting industrial unrest, until the German attack on Russia in 1941, when they somersaulted over-night and announced that the war was after all in defence of democracy and the ordinary people of Britain. But

A few mavericks

139

Bevan, editor of the left-wing *Tribune*, and strong critic of the coalition Government, defends the freedom of the Press at the meeting of the National Council for Civil Liberties in 1942

the Labour Movement was never seriously divided, as it had been in the previous war, and resolutions against continuing participation in the Coalition never received more than a handful of votes at Conference. The rank and file was solidly, though not jingoistically as some were in 1914, behind Attlee and his colleagues in the common pursuit of victory.

Policies for post-war reconstruction

Although immersed in the immediate military struggle against Hitler, Labour politicians did not lose sight of the purpose of battle. 'If we really wish to build a new world,' declared Attlee in a wartime broadcast, 'wherein justice, mercy and truth shall replace brute force, wherein equality and good neighbourliness shall take the place of violence, aggression and domination, we must also build a new Britain.' The National Executive was already planning to this end in 1942 and 1943, when it published comprehensive programmes for better housing and education. From within the Government Bevin saw through his Catering Wages Act and Dalton his measure for relocating industry into depressed areas. Ministers, Labour as well as Conservative, appeared less enthusiastic about the Beveridge Committee Report in 1942 with its sweeping proposals for social security 'from the cradle to the grave'. But nearly every Labour MP not in the Government voted for more urgent attention to the social services and subsequently Beveridge's schemes were absorbed into Labour's programme, undoubtedly leaving the impression that Labour cared more than the Conservatives about reconstructing a better post-war Britain.

July election

Germany surrendered on 7 May 1945. Churchill, contrary to general expectations and his own previous promises, now proposed to Attlee that the Coalition should continue until the defeat of Japan; failing this, he threatened an immediate election. The Labour Conference in session at Blackpool rejected both these alternatives and urged an election in the autumn, thereby giving the country and especially the forces time to prepare. But Churchill, pressed by his Conservative advisors to cash in quickly on his popularity as the great war victor, brought the Coalition to a hasty end and announced a July election. The politicians so recently colleagues in the Cabinet now found themselves attacking one another on the hustings, where they were joined by many candidates arrived straight from the batttefields in uniform.

The 1945 election, where many candidates and their helpers came fresh from the battlefields

Nearly everybody was convinced that the Conservatives, or at least Churchill, would win the election. 'Whatever exuberant rhetoric may from time to time pretend,' wrote one commentator during the campaign, 'nobody seriously thinks that the Labour Party have any chance of gaining a clear majority at the election.' Even Attlee, possibly impressed by the cheering crowds which greeted Churchill's electoral cavalcade, later admitted that he had privately expected the Tories to pull it off. The results started coming in early on 26 July. Among the first was the defeat of Harold Macmillan at Stockton-on-Tees. Before the day was out thirteen senior Conservative Ministers had fallen. It was a landslide. Labour had received twelve and a quarter million votes, many of them from middle-class suburbia, and over two million more than the Conservatives. Helped by distortions in the constituency system, the party had won 393 seats, giving it an overall majority of some 150.

In subsequent analyses, some observers argued that Labour had won because of its superior electoral organization, or because its manifesto, *Let Us Face the Future*, had promised a more attractive programme of social and economic reform, or because 'the forces went solidly left'. But even if these explanations of Labour's advantages were true – and they are disputable – their effects could only have been marginal. Much more important was that the British people in 1945 voted against the dismal pre-war past and 'the guilty men', the Tories, who were held to be responsible for the misery of those times. 'There was,' as Lord Kilmuir, a Conservative Lord Chancellor, later reflected, 'a profound and burning determination in the electorate never to go back to 1939.' There was also a deep desire to go forward to a better world and a belief that only Labour, the party of progress, could be trusted to keep its promises and avoid the betrayals which had followed the First World War. Not even Churchill could save the Tories. Never a real Conservative Party man, he had been rejected by them in the 1930s when his realism was most needed. In 1945 it was perfectly reasonable to cheer for Churchill and to vote for Attlee, whose team had proved its fitness to govern in the Coalition and now offered genuine hope of building a better Britain.

Clement Attlee and his wife acknowledge the cheers of supporters as they arrive at Transport House after the election victory

Clement Attlee drove to the Palace in his little pre-war Austin to accept the King's commission to form the first Labour Government with a majority in the Commons. He was strengthened by being able to call upon a sizeable group of Ministers already experienced in office. The key figures in his Cabinet were to be Bevin, as Foreign Secretary over-seeing the whole field of foreign affairs, including colonies, Morrison, as Lord President charged with co-ordinating all of the domestic programme, and Dalton at the Exchequer. The Prime Minister himself, the epitome of middle-class respectability and integrity and everybody's idea of a good chairman, maintained, beneath a deceptively mild exterior, a firm supervision of policies and personalities. At times there were demands for more personal initiative from the top and even a

Attlee's Government

The Attlee Government, 1945. *Seated:* Lord Addison, Lord Jowitt, Sir Stafford Cripps, Arthur Greenwood, E. Bevin, C. R. Attlee, H. Morrison, H. Dalton, A. V. Alexander, Chuter Ede, E. Wilkinson, *Standing:* A. Bevan, G. Isaacs, Lord Stansgate, G. H. Hall, Lord Pethick-Lawrence, J. J. Lawson, J. Westwood, E. Shinwell, T. E. Williams, Tom Williams

move led by Cripps in 1947 to replace Attlee. But while Bevin gave his unwavering loyalty, the leadership was never in serious doubt. The Government presented a strong team, representing all sections of the movement and probably the most personally capable and politically formidable to hold office in peacetime since 1918. For the first few years it easily dominated the Opposition in the Commons. Behind it, the new Parliamentary Labour Party which gathered triumphantly after the election, two-thirds of them in the Commons for the first time, was strikingly different from the solidly working-class party of 1906. It contained a large contingent of young professional men, teachers, doctors, lawyers and even businessmen. Only one-third were sponsored by the trade unions – a percentage that was to remain constant for the next twenty years.

Labour had fought the election on an enormous and detailed programme of reforms in all spheres of national life and the Government was remarkably successful in carrying them through. Its most popular measures naturally concerned the social services. Beveridge's schemes for comprehensive social insurance were implemented by a string of legislation in the years 1945–8 and Nye Bevan, Attlee's surprise but successful choice for Minister of Health, introduced the National Health Service, perhaps the most urgent and farreaching of all Labour's reforms. In education, the schoolleaving age was raised to fifteen, fees were abolished in local authority primary and secondary schools, and scholarships to universities were greatly expanded. By its legislation for town and country planning, for New Towns and for National Parks, the Government showed a proper socialist concern for the quality of people's living environment.

Aneurin Bevan, the Minister of Health, inspecting house construction (*top left*), and (*right*) meeting a United States Congressman, visiting England to study the British National Health Service, which was introduced by Bevan and based on the proposals of the wartime Beveridge Report

Much of Labour's nationalization programme was also enacted with surprisingly little difficulty, for the nation recognized that such apparently partizan proposals had very practical justifications in view of the need for investment and modernization on a scale beyond the capacity of private enterprise. Coal and the railways, two inefficient and unprofit able industries, were smoothly taken over by 1948, as were the airlines, electricity and gas, each of which was already subject to substantial public regulation. The Conservatives in Parliament and the Press reserved their main opposition for road haulage and iron and steel, both of which were profitable and not alarmingly inefficient. Moreover, several Labour Ministers, including Morrison, were themselves uncer tain about the form and priority to be given to steel nationalization. The Cabinet dithered over possible compromises and the bill was not finally drafted and passed till 1949. By then Labour had lost some of its initial momentum and the House of Lords, beginning again to assert itself as a brake on radical change, forced the Government to delay the vesting date until 1951.

Although these social and industrial reforms gave most satisfaction to Labour supporters, it was economic and financial questions which mattered most immediately to the fate of the Government and the nation. The Labour Government of 1945–51 began and ended in a financial crisis and the extent of its social progress was at all times circumscribed by the terrible realities of Britain's post war economic position. The cost of the war had been enormous, much higher pro portionately than to any other Western ally. Britain's overseas invest ments had been reduced by one third and she had incurred debts of over £3,000 million. The deficit on the balance of payments in 1945 was running at £1,200 million, far more than her total gold and currency reserves, and made worse by the sudden cessation of American lend lease aid after Japan's surrender. Bankruptcy faced Dalton when he took over the Exchequer and an extraordinary effort was required to restore economic viability, let alone prosperity. The nation's capital equipment was in a poor condition from which to base such a recovery, for in dustrial plant was badly run down owing to lack of maintenance and replacement in the war. Enemy action had sunk half of Britain's

Emanuel Shinwell, the Minister of Fuel and Power, who nationalized the coal mines, at the first National Coal Board Exhibition. Bevan, an ex-miner, is on the extreme right

merchant marine tonnage and destroyed or damaged four and a half million homes, one-third of the national total.

The first essential step towards recovery were large loans from the *Economic* United States and Canada to tide over the immediate crisis. Labour's *recovery* left wing immediately objected to incurring financial obligations to capitalist America and they joined the Tory right wing in voting against the loan. But it was clear to the large majority of M Ps and observers that without the loan, not only would Labour lack the resources to carry out her promised social reforms, but the country would have to suffer an immediate and severe reduction in its living standards. Given this breathing space the Government was able to work for longer term economic recovery. Under Dalton this was pursued through cheapening interest rates to encourage investment and retaining the machinery of war-time controls to insure that resources were allocated where most needed. But Dalton's unquenchable optimism allowed the economy to

147

run into inflationary pressures. The fuel crisis during the terrible winter of 1946–7 and the run on the pound after sterling had been made freely convertible in the following summer added to the economic difficulties. By the autumn of 1947 emergency measures had to be taken: the weekly meat ration was reduced to 1s. 2d., bacon to two ounces and sugar to half a pound. This crisis marked a watershed for the Labour Government. Until then, buoyed by its great electoral victory, cushioned by the American loan and facing only weak opposition in Parliament or in the country, it had pressed on with almost euphoric confidence. Henceforward it lived in constant awareness of the country's perilous economic circumstances.

Sir Stafford Cripps, who had moved from his earlier political extremism to a position of austere orthodoxy, replaced Dalton at the Exchequer and attempted to introduce a more fully planned economy. Annual Economic Surveys were published setting out the general economic objectives of the Government and a central planning staff allocated production and export targets accordingly. Cripps was greatly helped by a policy of wage restraint voluntarily applied by the trade unions. Considerable success was achieved and by 1950 it could fairly be said that Labour had re-established the economy from the bankruptcy of war. Exports had been raised to one hundred and seventy-five per cent of pre-war volume and shortly Britain was able to renounce

The fuel crisis: queueing for coke outside a gas works in the East End of London in the winter of 1947

(Left) The Chancellor of the Exchequer, Hugh Dalton, on Budget Day 1947. Cripps *(right)* succeeded him as Chancellor later that year when Dalton unintentionally 'leaked' the contents of his autumn budget to the Press and had to resign

further American Marshall Plan aid. But the margin of success was still very fine and insufficient to give protection from unfavourable international trading conditions. In 1949 an American recession and the resulting drop in Britain's exports forced Cripps to devalue the pound. Two years later world inflation, consequent on the Korean War, once more produced a sterling crisis.

Labour's economic situation, from the American loan to the Korean crisis, was closely related to its position in foreign affairs and particularly to the conflict between Russia and the West. Britons of all parties had felt and displayed genuine goodwill towards Russia during her great war effort against Hitler. In the General Election of 1945, Labour claimed, sincerely if naïvely, that it could best deal amicably with Russia since, as Bevin said, Left could speak best with Left. But this goodwill dissipated in most quarters as Stalin proved intransigent on all questions of post-war discussion and maintained an iron grip on the East European countries he had captured at the end of the war. Russian pressure

Communist threats

on Greece, Turkey and Iran, the blockade of Berlin and the coup in Czechoslovakia revealed Stalin's ambitions to extend his communist empire. As the cold war intensified, Bevin, realizing Britain's and Europe's weakness, made Anglo-American co-operation the keystone of his policies. He saw conscription introduced at home and worked to further the Marshall Plan of economic aid to Europe and the NATO effort to co-ordinate military defence.

This defensive alliance with America led, perhaps inevitably, to disagreements within the Party. Traditional pacifists opposed all alliances and armaments, as they had done in 1914–18 and in the 1930s. A few MPs clearly believed that Russia was always right and America always wrong. A larger and more significant group marched under the banner 'Keep Left' and spoke through *Tribune* and the *New Statesman*, demanding a 'socialist third force' policy, independent of both America and Russia, but prior to 1950 they were not obsessively anti-American and rarely formed a serious threat to the unity of the Party. Moreover these same divergent groups were often united and conciliated by the Government's record in colonial affairs, where the granting of independence to India, Pakistan and Ceylon formed the core of a new British Commonwealth of Nations in Asia and ranked as historic acts of statesmanship. Repressive action in Palestine alone marred this colonial record and strained party loyalties at all levels.

British troops maintaining order in Palestine were both victims and perpetrators of savage violence. Bevin's handling of this tragic situation was subject to wide criticism

Crisis between East and West: the RAF airlifts supplies to Berlin, blockaded by the Russians in 1948

The NATO Council meets in London to discuss defence, 1950. Bevin is sitting upper left

Indians, having been granted independence, bid an affectionate farewell to the Mountbattens, the last Viceroys of India

Coventry city centre after the raids in 1940

The old East End of London in 1946

In February 1950 the Labour Government was able to go to the country with an outstanding record of reform and reconstruction achieved. It had restored the British economy, built a welfare state which gave people the right to education, health and security, established a fairer society more in tune with the egalitarian twentieth century, and striven to defend democracy abroad and to settle international problems by international negotiation. Unemployment, the scourge of the working people in this century, had been banished, never rising above 1·8 per cent since demobilization was completed. Labour could be reasonably optimistic about facing the electorate since throughout its five years of government it had not lost a single by-election. In the General Election, however, although it raised its vote to thirteen and a quarter million votes, the highest total till then achieved by a party in Britain and three quarters of a million more than the Conservatives, its share of the poll fell slightly and its number of seats fell sharply to 315. It was left with an overall majority of only six.

Post-war reconstruction: Coventry as it has been rebuilt

Prospective Labour M Ps canvassing in their constituencies, 1950: Ian Nicholson in Argyle in Scotland (*above*) and A. E. Stubbs in Cambridgeshire (*below*)

Labour election posters of 1950

Several plausible reasons have been suggested to explain Labour's *The 1950 election stalemate* sudden decline from the great heights of 1945. For a start the electoral system, previously in Labour's favour, had been changed significantly to Labour's disadvantage by the redistribution of seats. The timing of the election in the depths of winter, shortly after the 1949 economic crisis and devaluation, may also have worked against Labour. Herbert Morrison argued that a delay until the summer weather when the economy was booming and Labour's full vote could have been turned out would have benefited the Party. These two technical factors alone may have been sufficient to deprive Labour of the small margin of extra votes and seats needed for Parliamentary safety. But other more important forces may well have worked against Labour. Having achieved its great programme, the Party offered little new to the nation; it stood on its excellent past record, a radical party beginning to appeal to conservative instincts. By 1950 also the British people, and especially the middle-classes who then defected back to the Tories, were undoubtedly hankering for less austerity and central direction and for more individual freedom to indulge in the consumer revolution then about to break on Western Europe. Under Labour they had nobly minded and sown the

155

seed corn. They now wished to relax a little and enjoy some of the harvest. But Labour often gave the impression that, having been so concerned with solving the problems of past scarcity, it did not fully recognize and understand this new movement towards future individual affluence. The electorate had certainly not rejected Labour – not yet anyway. Its judgment was ambiguous. But the closeness of the result meant that in the new Parliament the Government would be able to achieve little. Ten years of participating in strong and fruitful government was over. Labour still had a precarious hold on office, but the slide from power back into the wilderness was about to begin.

Attlee greeting an elector in his constituency

Chapter Ten

LEAN YEARS AGAIN

For eighteen months the Government survived on its tiny majority without finding a new momentum. The completion of steel nationalization was Labour's only controversial measure. For the most part, the Parliamentary stalemate was accepted as a check on bold new measures. But in any case, the Party could find no ready formula for a convincing programme either of legislation or for the next General Election. The nationalization of sugar and cement, which had been included in the 1950 Manifesto, were quietly dropped. In the first half of 1950, the economy was in excellent shape, with production, exports and reserves at record levels; and at the end of the year it proved possible to dispense with Marshall Aid. But as 1951 came in, the dominating facts were the deteriorating balance of payments problem, the high cost of the Korean War and sharply rising prices.

In the House of Commons and in the country the mood of the Party worsened. In October 1950, Stafford Cripps, borne down by illness, was replaced as Chancellor of the Exchequer by Hugh Gaitskell. Six months later, illness also forced the retirement from the Foreign Office of Ernest Bevin and the appointment of Herbert Morrison in his place. These changes did not please Aneurin Bevan, who was disappointed at being passed over for promotion and fiercely unwilling to accept the new Chancellor's view of the ceiling for health service expenditure.

157

(*Left*) Stafford Cripps, 62, and suffering ill-health. (*Right*) Herbert Morrison, the new Foreign Secretary, and Hugh Gaitskell, the new Chancellor of the Exchequer

Bevan resigns   Although he had now moved to the Ministry of Labour, he fought tenaciously against the imposition of charges on false teeth and spectacles, calculated to save £25 million a year. At a later stage, the massive increase in defence expenditure, which was the dominating feature of the 1951 Budget, became the main object of his criticism. In April he resigned, taking with him Harold Wilson, President of the Board of Trade, and John Freeman, a junior minister. By the autumn he had become the acknowledged leader of the left and the Party was seen to be openly and gravely split.

To the economic problem and internal controversy was added a crisis over Persian oil. On this and other foreign office matters Herbert Morrison showed a much less sure touch than in his long tenure of responsibility at home. And in the House of Commons, the difficulties of governing were intensified by constant harassing from a Conservative Opposition that was sniffing power once again.

In October 1951 Clement Attlee decided to break the stalemate. It was the worst possible moment to choose for a General Election, but in the event the Labour Party's vote was not only larger than in the previous year, it was the largest in British history. Its margin over the Conservatives, however, was reduced. Owing to the very heavy preponderance of Labour voters in some constituencies, for which Labour's own Redistribution Act was responsible, the Party had a built-in electoral disadvantage in the country as a whole. The shift of opinion was decisive: the precarious balance of the previous Parliament was upset. A Conservative Government returned with a majority of seventeen seats over the other parties. For the first time since 1940 Labour was wholly out of power.

Harold Wilson, formerly President of the Board of Trade, and Aneurin Bevan, who had both resigned from the Government earlier in the year, with three other left-wingers, Ian Mikardo, Tom Driberg and Barbara Castle, at the 1951 Party Conference

A loss of momentum after six successful but wearing years was to be expected. The Labour Party had carried out the greater part of its 1945 programme in difficult domestic and international circumstances. The strain of office, continuous for some of its leaders from the war years, had killed two of its principal figures, Ernest Bevin and Stafford Cripps. A major social revolution had been achieved and the country had survived the stern task of economic reconstruction. A breathing space, both for the Party and the people, was required.

But the Party itself could not take such an objective view of events. Since the disappointment of 1950, dissatisfaction had been growing with the uncertain sense of direction of the leadership. The resignation of Aneurin Bevan and his colleagues had been a symptom of the rivalries and disagreement at the top. In the country, the separate groups whose unity in good times gave the Party strength began to pull apart. Conflicts between the practical men and the visionaries, the pragmatists and the doctrinaries, had been commonplace in the past, particularly in the years before 1914 and 1939. Now, with doubt and disillusionment, they came once more to matter. The defeat of 1951 opened the flood-gates of recrimination. Thirteen long years were to pass, and much self-inflicted damage was to be done, before Labour was back in power again.

Winston Churchill mobbed on polling day

The first weekend when petrol was sold off ration, May 1950

The problems of the 1950s were not, however, all or even fundamentally of the Labour Party's own making. Changing economic and social circumstances, towards which the Party's successful post-war period of office substantially contributed, cut at the roots of Labour's traditional support.

In 1938, the last full year before the war, nearly two million men and women, 13·5 per cent of the working population, had been unemployed; in 1951 not much over a quarter of a million, 1·2 per cent of the working population, were without jobs. Despite fluctuations during periods of economic recession over the country as a whole, full employment had become the rule. Increases in earnings outstripped the rise in prices. In real terms, standards of living rose more between 1951 and 1959 than in the twenty-five years between 1913 and 1938. The number of private cars on the road doubled in eight years. Increased opportunities in education were another sign of the times. Before the war there had been fewer than 50,000 full time university students, only a small proportion supported from public funds. By the late 1950s there were twice as many, and the great majority were on scholarships. To the traditional Labour voter, now perhaps in a white-collar trade union, living in a new house with a garage, his children earning good money or going on to higher education, it was a very different prospect from that which had faced the pioneers fifty years earlier.

Architects of Conservative revival: Harold Macmillan is met by R.A. Butler on his return to England from Africa, where he had made his celebrated 'wind of change' speech in 1960

Conservatives
and change

The change was not lost on the Conservatives. They had taken their defeat in 1945 as a challenge to modernize their party and ideas. Most of all they were determined to throw off the dismal image of the 1930s, to turn their backs on the days of unemployment and of Munich. Coming into power at a time when post-war difficulties were easing, they were able finally to end irksome rationing and controls and to preside over a rapid rise in living standards. To the electorate they appeared as a party of moderate reform, preserving the larger part of Labour's post-war achievement and responding pragmatically to cross-currents of fresh thinking. Before and during Winston Churchill's period as Prime Minister, and under the wing of his Chancellor of the Exchequer, R. A. Butler, a flexible philosophy of Toryism was evolved. Later during the skilful premiership of Harold Macmillan a leadership team emerged, younger and more representative than hitherto. Against this background and as in the heyday of Liberal England between 1906 and 1914, the Labour Party found it hard to present a constructive alternative to win over the body of middle opinion essential to electoral success. A major effort was required if Labour was to demonstrate again its fitness to govern.

162

But the need to adapt was not immediately grasped by the majority of active members of the Party. There was scepticism about whether prosperity had come to stay and new policies provoked misgivings. The Party had become set in its ways, conservative at a time when the Conservative Party had begun to welcome and even hasten change. A substantial element in its membership refused to acknowledge an economic and social environment very different from the 1930s, and declined to modify its traditional approach to the electorate. The rambling structure of the Party militated against a quick response to leadership. In any case, the leadership itself was divided on crucial issues.

For much of the 1950s the strains in the Party were reflected in the clash between Hugh Gaitskell and Aneurin Bevan. It was already clear in 1951 that a new generation of top leaders would soon be required. In particular, the choice of a successor to Clement Attlee could not be long postponed. Gaitskell and Bevan were the obvious candidates and their rivalry was sharpened by temperamental differences and mutual antagonism. In their background and approach to politics, Gaitskell and Bevan were representative of two vital elements that had helped to mould the Party. Gaitskell, the son of an Indian Civil Servant, educated at Winchester and New College, was a Fabian intellectual. He had joined the Labour Party at the time of the General Strike and had been a university teacher during the 1930s. The main-spring of his socialism was a passionate belief both in social justice and in personal freedom. In politics he was a pragmatist, applying a keen and logical mind to the solution of practical problems.

Gaitskell versus Bevan

Bevan came from very different stock. He had been born and brought up in the Monmouthshire mining community of Tredegar. After leaving school at thirteen, and going on a scholarship to the London Labour College, he had learned politics the hard way in the harsh class conflicts of the valleys. By the 1950s Bevan was much more a self-educated intellectual than a typical product of working-class trade unionism. But the firmness of his roots in South Wales and his position on the left of the Party before and during the war put him in a sharp contrast to Gaitskell. He was a formidable alternative candidate for the

In April 1954 Bevan resigned from the Shadow Cabinet and (*right*) in October he spoke against the official
line on German rearmament at the Party Conference

Arthur Deakin

leadership with his seniority in Parliament and the positive achievement
of the National Health Service on his side.

As it happened, the struggle for power took four years and a heavy
toll of the Party's standing in the country. In 1952 'the Bevanites' made
an almost clean sweep of the constituency section of the National
Executive Committee, defeating Herbert Morrison and Hugh Dalton.
The Bevanite weekly *Tribune*, brilliantly edited and sold in the manner
of the old *Clarion* by devoted supporters, carried on a strenuous campaign
against the right-wing leadership. While Bevanite teams of 'Brains
Trusts' toured the country, Gaitskell hit back by accusing the Bevanites
of attempting mob rule and playing into the hands of a Communist
minority. The leaders of the great trade unions, particularly Arthur
Deakin of the Transport Workers and Tom Williamson of the General
and Municipal Workers, demanded loyalty to majority decisions and
an end to the factionalism of the left. A severe strain was put on the
always-difficult relationship between the trade unions and the constituencies. The alliance of Bradford looked as if it might break as trade
union leaders, now with ready access to Downing Street even under a

On his election as Treasurer of the Labour Party, Hugh Gaitskell is congratulated by Herbert Morrison

Conservative Government, grew impatient of rank-and-file Bevanism. The Bevanites in the constituencies in turn were increasingly incensed by the 'bloc vote' of the unions which was thrown against them at the annual Party Conference.

At the October 1954 Conference they came near to defeating the leadership on the issue of the rearmament of Germany to which many others, normally on the right wing of the Party, were opposed. But in the main they remained a vocal and militant group commanding per-haps a quarter of the Parliamentary Labour Party although a majority in the constituency parties. *German rearmament*

The Conference which debated German rearmament also saw a turning point in the struggle for power between Bevan and Gaitskell. The office of Party Treasurer, normally a sinecure, became vacant and with the backing of the main trade unions, Gaitskell beat Bevan for it by a majority of almost two to one. For the first time he sat on the National Executive Committee and began to win in the country the reputation he had already earned in Parliament. Bevan, on the other hand, lost his seat in choosing, unnecessarily, to fight for the Treasurer's

165

office. At the 1955 Conference, Gaitskell was re-elected Treasurer with an overwhelming majority over Bevan and took the opportunity of a Conference platform to make a dramatic affirmation of personal faith. When, two months later, Clement Attlee resigned as leader of the Party, Gaitskell was elected his successor. He polled 157 votes to Bevan's 70, with Herbert Morrison trailing in third place with 40.

*Hugh Gaitskell
elected leader*

The marks of the bitter struggle were not easily erased. The argument over the leadership was not the only element in the internal controversy, and the issues which lay behind the struggle remained unresolved. The relevance and rate of extension of nationalization was a divisive question. Was public ownership a means towards socialism or was it socialism itself? The debate echoed down from the formative years, but this time it was conducted in the full glare of publicity by a party seriously seeking to win votes. Overshadowing all was the question of whether a capitalist economy, managed by Keynesian techniques, could now avoid serious crises and offer steady prosperity. Defence and foreign affairs brought out other, long-standing tensions. Apart from the debates first on British then on German rearmament, defence policy in South-East Asia provoked a clash which, in 1954, resulted in Bevan's resignation from the Shadow Cabinet. In 1955 there was the first of many differ-ences on the Party's attitude towards nuclear weapons. Labour found it hard to accept the brutal facts of a divided world in which power rather than international law still played the predominant part.

It was hardly a surprise, in the circumstances, when the General Election in May 1955 left the Conservatives more firmly in the saddle with a majority increased from seventeen to sixty. Labour's vote in the country fell by a million and a half. It was a sobering defeat.

Once Hugh Gaitskell had been elected leader later in the year, a slow process of internal healing began. The Party organization in the country, tuned to a fine pitch in the early days by Arthur Henderson, but long since neglected, was the subject of a searching enquiry by Harold Wilson. The modernization of the machine was followed by constructive discussions on policy, particularly in the fields of traditional concern to the Labour Party: education and pensions. There was a new readiness to consider ideas on their merits and less of a tendency to

Election posters, 1955

A deputation representative of the Labour Party, TUC and Co-operative Movement arrives at the Soviet Embassy to protest about Hungary in 1956

Hugh Gaitskell at the time of his election as leader of the Labour Party, 1955

attach pejorative labels to the unacceptable. In 1952 *New Fabian Essays* had attempted to do for the 1950s what the original *Fabian Essays* had done in 1889, and in the same year Aneurin Bevan had published his testament *In Place of Fear*. But the events of the Labour Government were too close and the mood of the Party was not receptive. The later 1950s saw a change. Labour Party and Fabian pamphlets were increasingly read and *The Future of Socialism* by C.A.R. Crosland, the most thorough and intellectually distinguished statement of 'revisionist' socialism, had a profound influence even on those hostile to its theme. The suppression by Russian tanks of the Hungarian rising late in 1956 produced a wholesale exodus from the British Communist Party and a wave of discussion on the 'new left', especially amongst young people. New ideas were no longer at a discount either on the right or left of the Party.

Fresh thinking

Unity restored Personal differences, however, were not so readily overcome. But gradually through 1956 and 1957 Aneurin Bevan moved into a closer working partnership with Hugh Gaitskell, detaching himself from the less responsible critics on the left. The Conservative Government's Suez operation at the end of 1956 united the Labour Party for the first time for almost twenty years in a passionate protest over an issue of foreign policy. At the 1957 Party Conference Bevan found it possible to join with the rest of the leadership even on the sensitive question of Britain's possession of the hydrogen bomb. Unity was helped by the obvious decline in the fortunes of the Conservative Government, which the Suez disaster appeared to accelerate. It looked as if Labour was at last firmly on the road back to power.

Mass Labour rally in Trafalgar Square against Government action in invading Suez, November 1956. Bevan addressed the meeting

Chapter Eleven

CRISIS AND RECOVERY

By early 1958 the unpopularity of the Conservative Government was showing in by-election and local election results and a handsome lead for Labour in opinion polls. It seemed as if the lean years were over and that the General Election would bring a harvest of Parliamentary seats. In the eighteen months that followed, this rich promise withered away. The Labour Party in Parliament, and to a substantial extent in the trade unions and constituencies, was united in putting across a coherent and apparently attractive programme. The face which the Party presented to the electorate was less traditional and doctrinaire than at any time in years. The election campaign was a model of planning and precision in which much of the popularity lost in the preceding months appeared to be regained. But when polling day came, Labour lost seats and a Conservative Government returned with an overall majority increased to one hundred. For the first time since the Reform Bill of 1832, a party had won three successive General Elections and improved its position on each occasion.

This unprecedented victory for the Conservatives was an unprecedented blow to Labour. 'Can Labour survive?' was now the crucial question. The appeal of a party still believed to stand mainly for the working class (and to be the political arm of the trade unions) was waning as more and more voters ceased to identify themselves with the

Despite much re-thinking of policy the Labour Party made little headway against the securely established image of Conservative prosperity

Lost loyalties under-privileged. The old age pensioners alone seemed loyal to their long-standing allegiance. Nationalization, a distinctively Labour policy, was unpopular even with settled Labour voters. With the rapidly rising ownership of homes, cars, television sets and washing machines, neither Labour's welfare policies nor its economic plans appeared to be relevant. The Conservative election slogan 'You've never had it so good' had been effective because for most people it had been true; and the corollary, 'Don't let Labour ruin it', had struck a chord in memories of post-war austerity and hardship. The problem for the Party now was whether it could change its public image while retaining a distinctive socialist approach. Could it prove itself to be an undoctrinaire party of conscience and reform concerned with efficiency as well as welfare and yet provide a clear alternative to the Conservatives ?

The debate within the Party revived in public all the divisions and bitterness of the Bevanite controversy. It was soon carried over into a fierce struggle about defence policy which had little to do with the main question of modernization but was another symptom of the disappointment and frustration of a crushing electoral defeat.

Of the various drastic solutions proposed to end the Party's dilemma, Hugh Gaitskell at once rejected the possibility of an alliance with the Liberals (whose six seats in the House of Commons concealed a potential of perhaps three million votes) or a change of name and a break with the trade unions. But amongst his proposals for modernization was one designed to make clear that Labour accepted a mixed economy and that nationalization was one of several means to socialism, not an end in itself. Clause Four of the Constitution, specifying the Party's objective as 'to secure for the workers by hand or by brain the full fruits of their industry . . . upon the basis of the common ownership of the means of production, distribution and exchange', dated from Sidney Webb's draft of forty years before. Hugh Gaitskell proposed to change this definition in order not only to put nationalization into the perspective of Labour's total programme but also to demonstrate the Party's determination to bring itself up to date.

(*Right*) The public ownership controversy: James Callaghan arrives for a National Executive Committee meeting to consider revising the controversial Clause 4 of the Labour Party constitution, March 1960

(*Below*) 'Mods' on the left, 'rockers' on the right, one symptom of confused attitudes amongst young people in an affluent society

The change was, predictably, strenuously opposed by the left of the Party but did not find favour either with a substantial section of the right and centre which normally supported the leadership. In the event a compromise statement of additional Party objectives was agreed on and Clause Four itself remained unamended. The Party had been forced into critical self-examination and a realistic reappraisal of its principles. It was more clear-headed as a result. But in the short run old wounds had been reopened and the authority of Hugh Gaitskell diminished.

In the Clause Four controversy Aneurin Bevan played little part. A conciliatory and unifying speech made at the 1959 post-election Conference was almost his last. After a long illness he died in the summer of 1960 at a time when his personal influence and his acceptance of Hugh Gaitskell's leadership might have steadied the Party. Three years before, in an early debate on nuclear weapons, he had warned the Party against 'going naked into the Conference chamber'. Now, in his absence, the demand was growing for unilateral disarmament.

Unilateral disarmament
That the left wing of the Party and the pacifists should find themselves in opposition to the leadership on defence and foreign affairs was not new. But on this occasion they were joined by a larger number, deeply worried by the threat of nuclear warfare and anxious to find a simple solution to the complex problem of a peaceful settlement to world

Anti-H bomb demonstrators marching from Aldermaston to London in what became an annual Easter demonstration

Hugh Gaitskell opposes unilateral disarmament in the 1960 Scarborough Conference

tensions. There were, in addition, those who were reluctant for personal reasons (including his attempt to change Clause Four) actively to assist Hugh Gaitskell. Most important of all, the largest trade union, the Transport and General Workers, could no longer be relied upon to cast its massive vote in support of the leadership. On the contrary, its General Secretary, Frank Cousins, unlike his predecessors, was a vigorous spokesman of the left. In the country as a whole, the highly organized Campaign for Nuclear Disarmament aroused public opinion through skilful propaganda, including its annual Aldermaston March. To its energetic work in constituency Labour parties and trade unions was added the disruptive activities of Communists and other fringe groups out to serve their own particular purposes. At the Scarborough Conference in October 1960 a resolution supporting unilateral disarmament was narrowly carried despite a dramatic speech by Hugh Gaitskell.

Frank Cousins takes a different view, speaking against the platform and (*right*, rear) declining to applaud Gaitskell's speech

The crisis which now faced the Party was more acute even than that of a year earlier. In the Parliamentary Labour Party an overwhelming majority against unilateralism remained. Hugh Gaitskell's leadership was less secure but he was nevertheless re-elected with a vote of more than two to one over Harold Wilson, who was not a unilateralist but received unilateralist support. The doctrine of the independence of the Parliamentary Labour Party, first set out by Keir Hardie fifty years before, was re-asserted against the demand that 'Conference must decide'.

But a permanent breach between the Party in Parliament and the Party in the country was out of the question if Labour was to remain a serious candidate for office. Nor was it sufficient for the Party leader to command a majority of support amongst Labour MPs. There already seemed little chance of winning an election in 1964 and, unless unity was restored, the prospect even further ahead was bleak. A long debilitating conflict could destroy the Party altogether.

Then once again came a sudden reversal of fortune. The Party awoke to the consequences of its Scarborough decision. Previously unilateralism had seemed to be a peripheral issue, espoused as a good cause by a militant minority but no more critical for the Party than many others which had divided left and right. Now it appeared that, as Hugh Gaitskell had said, the survival of the Party itself was at stake. Abroad, amongst other social democratic parties, there was consternation at Labour's decision. More immediately disturbing, there was at home strong evidence that the public would decisively reject a party committed to unilateralism.

The first half of 1961 saw an intense campaign in the constituencies and the trade unions to reverse the Scarborough decision. The organization and propaganda of the Campaign for Nuclear Disarmament was matched by the strenuous efforts of Hugh Gaitskell's supporters. Rank-and-file members, who had been disheartened and outmanoeuvred by the unilateralists, now rallied and argued back. The leaders of the principal trade unions sought to bring their organizations into line behind Hugh Gaitskell and to redress the balance against the Transport and General Workers, still unequivocally committed on the other side.

The 1961 Conference applauds Gaitskell and the 1960 unilateralist decision is reversed

Two large unions, the Amalgamated Engineering Union and the Shopworkers (USDAW), were weaned from unilateralism and others followed suit. Well before the 1961 Conference it was clear that the previous year's decision would be reversed.

A change of heart

The reversal of the Scarborough decision was not only a symptom of a desire for unity and political survival as well as a triumph of organiza‚ tion; it also represented a change of heart. The initial success of uni‚ lateralism had been due to moral and political simplicity: Britain could lead the world to peace by renouncing the use of nuclear weapons. Now, on examination, unilateralism was seen also to involve an end to the NATO alliance which Ernest Bevin had created in the post‚war years as a counterpoise to the Soviet Union and her satellites. The policy of collective security would be abandoned, leaving Britain alone and without allies. But it was as unrealistic in the 1960s as it had been in 1914 and the 1930s to believe that moral gestures were a sufficient defence against weapons of war. *Policy for Peace*, the joint Labour Party and TUC statement on defence and disarmament agreed by the 1961 Conference, put the position succinctly:

We seek the banning of all nuclear weapons everywhere. But the West cannot renounce nuclear weapons so long as the Communist bloc possess them.

175

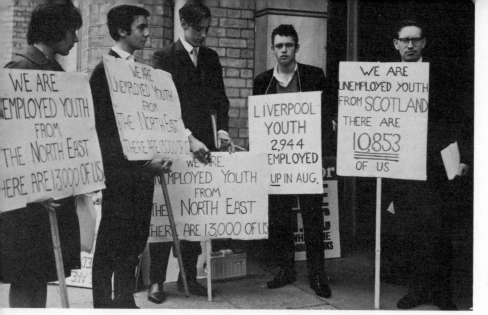

On the signs:

WE ARE EMPLOYED YOUTH FROM THE NORTH EAST THERE ARE 13,000 OF US

WE ARE UNEMPLOYED YOUTH FROM THE NORTH EAST THERE ARE 13,000 OF US

WE ARE UNEMPLOYED YOUTH FROM THE NORTH EAST THERE ARE 13,000 OF US

LIVERPOOL YOUTH 2,944 EMPLOYED UP IN AUG.

WE ARE UNEMPLOYED YOUTH FROM SCOTLAND THERE ARE 10,853 OF US

Unemployment rises to a post-war record in the winter of 1962-3

Unemployment

The debate on defence policy was not over, but from the end of 1961 it was no longer a crucial issue. Two new factors now combined to turn attention away from controversy within the Party to differences between the Conservative Government and Labour Opposition. In the first place, government measures to check inflation led to unemployment, which rose steadily from the autumn of 1961 until it reached a post-war peak in early 1963. Attempts by means of a 'pay pause' arbitrarily to restrain wage increases and to upset long-standing negotiating machinery, particularly affecting teachers and nurses, added to public discontent. This began to be reflected in a fall in support for the Government at by-elections, of which a dramatic Liberal victory at Orpington in March 1962 was a sign.

The Common Market

Secondly, the Government's decision to seek entry to the European Common Market provoked the Labour Party to a critical examination in Parliament of the likely terms of membership, and Hugh Gaitskell himself to outspoken opposition at the Brighton Conference. Opinion in the country appeared evenly balanced but hostility to entering the Common Market united the great majority of the Party and won back to Gaitskell many of those alienated by his stand on Clause Four and defence. The minority, principally on the right and centre of the Party, although influential, was not prepared to take its objection to the bitter point of a break.

176

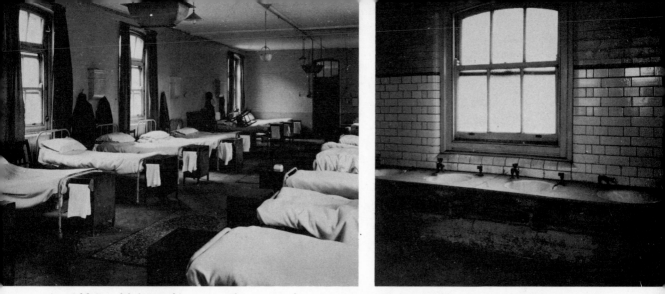

An Old People's 'Home' in 1961. The contrast between private affluence and inadequate spending on public services was a major criticism of the Conservative Government

By the end of 1962 the Party was in better heart than for years. The wounds were healing from which it had almost bled to death. The violence of internal argument had shocked it into a sober unity which was strengthened by the prospect that Conservative decline could, after all, mean a Labour victory next time. Hugh Gaitskell had come through fire and survived, accepted now – although reluctantly – by the left of the Party and achieving much support amongst uncommitted voters in the country.

But Hugh Gaitskell did not live to see the outcome of the recovery of the Party's fortunes. In January 1963, following a month's illness, he died of a rare disease at the age of fifty-six. He had had a long and painful *Gaitskell's* fight both to assert his authority over the Party and to change its image *death* with the electorate. More than anyone else he had become identified with the practical idealism required to make democratic socialism relevant and attractive in the mid-twentieth century. His death was a harsh blow.

In the election for leader that followed the candidates were George Brown, the Party's deputy leader since the death of Bevan, Harold Wilson, the principal figure on the left-centre of the Party, and James Callaghan, the 'Shadow' Chancellor of the Exchequer. Wilson won with a vote of 144 to Brown's 103 in the final ballot.

The new leader set out to consolidate the Party's improving position in the country and to complete the process of modernization. He retained the loyalty of Hugh Gaitskell's former closest colleagues, but could more readily command the support of the left of the Party. Profoundly bored by questions of ideology, he was a skilful party tactician and a most effective debater in the House of Commons. He had been educated at local council and grammar schools in the North of England, and had won a scholarship to Oxford. He had been a university lecturer, a civil servant and a Cabinet Minister at the age of thirty-one. Now, aged forty-seven, he was uncommonly fitted to appeal to the country as an undogmatic spokesman of a generation concerned at least as much with efficiency as welfare and anxious to escape from the restricting consequences of class distinctions and traditional national habits. At his first Party Conference, in the autumn of 1963, he took as the theme of his first speech the scientific revolution and the need to re-define socialism in the light of that revolution. It was a conclusive declaration that the cloth-capped party of Keir Hardie had gone for ever.

Labour's growing confidence was matched by the difficulties of the Conservative Government. A drastic reconstruction in the summer of

Harold Wilson, now leader of the Opposition, meets President Kennedy at the White House in 1963

The Wilson Cabinet in July 1965. *Seated:* William Ross, Secretary of State for Scotland; Sir Frank Soskice, Secretary of State for the Home Department; Michael Stewart, Secretary of State for Foreign Affairs; Lord Gardiner, the Lord Chancellor; George Brown, First Secretary of State and Minister for Economic Affairs; Harold Wilson, Prime Minister and First Lord of the Treasury; Herbert Bowden, Lord President of the Council; James Callaghan, Chancellor of the Exchequer; Denis Healey, Secretary of State for Defence; Arthur Bottomley, Secretary of State for Commonwealth Relations; James Griffiths, Secretary of State for Wales. *Standing:* Fred Lee, Minister of Power; Frank Cousins, Minister of Technology; Douglas Houghton, Chancellor of the Duchy of Lancaster; Anthony Crosland, Secretary of State for Education and Science; Douglas Jay, President of the Board of Trade; Barbara Castle, Minister of Overseas Development; Anthony Greenwood, Secretary of State for Colonial Affairs; the Earl of Longford, Lord Privy Seal; Richard Crossman, Minister of Housing and Local Government; Ray Gunter, Minister of Labour; Frederick Peart, Minister of Agriculture, Fisheries and Food; Thomas Fraser, Minister of Transport; Sir Burke Trend, Secretary to the Cabinet

1962, involving the dismissal of senior Ministers, was insufficient to prevent the erosion of support. The failure in January 1963 of the protracted negotiations for entry into the Common Market was followed by the Profumo scandal in June. Dissatisfaction with the leadership of Harold Macmillan, and his sudden illness, led in October to his replacement by Sir Alec Douglas-Home after a sharp contest that left the Party seriously divided. In the country by this time there was a profound disenchantment with the Conservatives and a feeling that they had lost the capacity for effective government. By 1964 the political situation promised a Labour victory comparable to that of 1945.

The 1964 election victory

But the election was postponed until the autumn when the Government's full five-year term expired, and by then the gap between the two parties had narrowed dramatically. The Liberals, fielding many more candidates than in 1959, took votes from both sides and almost doubled their share of the total poll. Labour made substantial gains from the Conservatives, and slightly increased its overall percentage; the Conservatives lost more in this one election than had Labour in the previous four together. Labour was left with a majority of thirteen seats over the Conservatives and four seats over the Conservatives and Liberals combined. It was a narrow squeak, but a remarkable victory in view of the size of the 1959 Conservative majority which had to be overturned. Allowing for the crisis of 1960, the drift to the Conservatives of more than a decade had been reversed in a little over three years. The long years of weariness, frustration and disappointment were over at last.

Harold Wilson formed the fourth Labour Government on 16 October 1964, but the narrowness of his majority immediately raised the question of whether Labour could effectively exercise power. Within a short time the loss of Leyton at a by-election held to provide a seat for the Foreign Secretary, Patrick Gordon Walker, threw further doubt on Labour's ability to carry on. There appeared to be a parallel with the 1950-1 Government which had achieved little except its own defeat.

Circumstances, however, proved to be different. From the beginning Harold Wilson made it clear that he intended to provide firm and purposeful government even on a tiny majority, and that there would be no running away from responsibility. In addition, whereas the current of public opinion in 1950-1 had been against the Government in power, evidence suggested that – despite Leyton – there was a continuing movement towards the Labour Party. It was widely felt that the new Government should be given a fair chance to show its paces. It was also quickly apparent that the Conservative Party, which changed its leader again in the summer of 1965, was having difficulty in adjusting to its new role in opposition and had no clear alternative policies to offer. The Opposition, in fact, began to show the signs of disunity which had been partly responsible for the downfall of Labour fifteen years before.

Harold Wilson showed skilful leadership, both in the House of Commons and in the country and quickly acquired an unusually high personal standing. At the same time the competence of the bulk of his team of ministers demonstrated to the electorate that Labour could govern. Younger ministers, like Roy Jenkins, were amongst those quick to make their mark.

The country did not expect immediate results, especially in view of the narrowness of Labour's majority. It was willing to applaud boldness and new ideas, even when they achieved only limited success. In particular, the Government made clear the priority it gave to tackling the nation's basic problem of economic growth. It had been elected at a time of crisis and inherited a very substantial balance of payments deficit from the previous Government. Nor was its own term of office free from times of acute concern about the balance of payments position.

Despite this, the Chancellor of the Exchequer, James Callaghan, carried through all its stages in the House of Commons a Finance Bill without precedent in its complexity. As part of a reorganization of the structure of government, a new Department of Economic Affairs was set up under George Brown which prepared and published a National Plan for economic development. Particular attention was given to the problem of preventing inflation while maintaining full employment by an active policy to deal with the relationship between productivity, prices and incomes. New machinery for regional planning was set up in order to secure a better balance of investment and employment between different parts of Britain.

In the field of social policy high priority was given to the needs of old age pensioners, and to housing. It was also decided that the future growth of public expenditure should be related to the growth of national wealth as set out in the National Plan.

The problems of the war in Vietnam and of Rhodesia involved the Prime Minister and the Foreign Secretary, Michael Stewart, in delicate negotiations abroad and careful handling of both the back benches and the Opposition in the House of Commons. Although a unilateral declaration of independence by Rhodesia was not avoided, there was a broad concensus that an exceedingly difficult international problem had been dealt with in the least dangerous way.

1966: Labour's decisive victory

By early 1966 the considerable record of legislation and indications, both at by-elections and in public opinion polls, that Labour would win, persuaded the Prime Minister to go to the country. The inescapable uncertainties of government on a narrow majority had convinced him that it was right to ask for a mandate to finish the job. Many problems – industrial efficiency, transport, local government reorganization – had so far proved intractable and needed continuing attention in an atmosphere free from electioneering pressures. It was also desirable to improve upon Labour's majority to ensure that the Government was fully heeded abroad as certain to speak for Britain for some time ahead.

The election mainly turned on the desirability of giving the Government a further, full, term to complete the work it had only just begun, and it demonstrated that a strong swing to Labour had occurred in the previous eighteen months. On polling day, 31 March, Labour received a majority of ninety-seven seats, and was decisively confirmed in power.

In eighty years the late Victorian England of the socialist pioneers had been transformed. Standards of living had been achieved for the working class which Hyndman, the Webbs, Hardie and Blatchford never dreamt were possible. The rigid lines of class had themselves been loosened as greater social mobility followed the growth and spread of wealth. From the beginning the Labour Party had been a broad coalition, embracing many divergent groups and widely differing opinions. But in the mainstream of the Party there had been a strong and continuing faith in democratic methods and political action. The pioneers had set out to achieve power by putting their own people into Parliament. They had used the freedom of the ballot box to win freedom from injustice, ugliness and squalor. During eighty years the Labour Movement had influenced society far in excess of its achievements during its periods in government. It had become a formidable factor in determining the face of Britain.

The Wilsons return triumphantly to 10 Downing Street, 1 April 1966 ▶

List of Illustrations

187

Select Bibliography

There are very many books on the history of the Labour Movement that the reader may wish to look at, although none satisfactorily covers the whole movement throughout the period.

For much useful background and narrative, two volumes in the Oxford History of England are important: *England 1870–1914* (1936) by R.C.K. ENSOR and *English History 1914–1945* (1965) by A.J.P. TAYLOR. Part of the period is similarly covered in C.L. MOWAT's excellent *Britain Between the Wars* (1955).

The formulative years are dealt with authoritatively in *The Origins of the Labour Party 1880–1900* (1954) by HENRY PELLING (from which the quotation at the end of Chapter I comes), *The Advent of the Labour Party* (1958) by PHILIP P. POIRER and *Labour and Politics 1900–1906* (1958) by FRANK BEALEY and HENRY PELLING. The *History of the Fabian Society* (2nd ed. 1916) by EDWARD R. PEASE covers the period up to 1914 and the *Story of Fabian Socialism* (1961) by MARGARET COLE covers virtually the whole period. The first volume of *A History of the Trade Unions since 1889* (1964) by H.A. CLEGG, ALAN FOX and A.F. THOMPSON takes events to 1910.

On the period before the 1880s, MARK HOVELL's *The Chartist Movement* (1918) is fifty years old but still worth reading. See also *Essays in Labour History* (1960) edited by ASA BRIGGS and JOHN SAVILLE and *The TUC 1868–1924* (1958) by B.C. ROBERTS. G.D.H. COLE's many contributions to Labour history include *A History of the Labour Party from 1914* (effectively, to 1945), 1948, and *A Short History of the British Working Class Movement* (2nd ed. 1937). FRANCIS WILLIAMS's *Fifty Years March* (1949) is detailed on the period from 1900 to 1918 but thin thereafter. HENRY PELLING's *Short History of the Labour Party* (from 1900), 2nd ed. 1965, is concise and up to date. A competent general history is *The British Labour Movement* by CARL F. BRAND (1965).

The Common People 1746–1946 (2nd ed. 1956) by G.D.H. COLE and RAYMOND POSTGATE is strong on economic and social background. For more detail see also the *Concise Economic History of Britain* (1954) by W.H.B. COURT, *The Condition of the British People 1911–1945* (1945) by MARK ABRAMS and *Survey of Social Conditions in England and Wales* (1952) by A.M. CARR SAUNDERS, D. CARADOG JONES and C. MOSER.

Autobiographies and biographies are a rich source of information (although sometimes a richer one of gossip). BEATRICE WEBB's *Our Partnership* (1948) and her two volumes of *Diaries* edited by MARGARET COLE covering 1912–1924 (1952) and 1924–1932 (1956) are valuable. HUGH DALTON's three volumes of *Memoirs* (1953–1962) are a more detailed record than any other published by a Labour politician, particularly on the 1930s and 1940s. C.R. ATTLEE is rather less forthcoming in *As It Happened* (1954) and, as told to Francis Williams, in *A Prime Minister Remembers* (1961).

Others are: EMRYS HUGHES, *Keir Hardie* (1956); LAURENCE THOMPSON, *Robert Blatchford* (1951); PHILIP SNOWDEN, *Autobiography* (1934); MARY AGNES HAMILTON, *Arthur Henderson* (1938); ALAN BULLOCK, *Ernest Bevin* (1960); HERBERT MORRISON, *An Autobiography* (1960); COLIN COOKE, *Stafford Cripps* (1957); LORD CITRINE, *Men and Work* (1964); MICHAEL FOOT, *Aneurin Bevan* (Vol. I, 1962); W.T. RODGERS (edited), *Hugh Gaitskell 1906–1963* (1964).

The Trouble Makers (1957) by A.J.P. TAYLOR is interesting on dissent and foreign policy up to 1939. On the problems of the inter-war years there are R.W. LYMAN, *The First Labour Government* (1957); JULIAN SYMONS, *The General Strike* (1957) and R. BASSETT, *Nineteen Thirty-One: Political Crisis* (1958). On the period after 1945 there is *Crisis in Britain 1951* (1963) by JOAN MITCHELL, and LESLIE HUNTER's *The Road to Brighton Pier* (1959), a graphic rather than scholarly account of internal troubles in the Labour Party in the 1950s.

Amongst other books are: R.T. McKENZIE, *British Political Parties* (2nd ed. 1963); MARTIN HARRISON, *Trade Unions and the Labour Party* (1960) and IVOR BULMER-THOMAS, *The Growth of the British Party System* (Vol. 2, 1965).

The *Annual Conference Reports* of the Labour Party document the story for most of the period.

Index